Quarterly Essay

Quarterly Essay is published four times a year by Black Inc., an imprint of Schwartz Books Pty Ltd. Publisher: Morry Schwartz.

ISBN 9781760642280 ISSN 1832-0953

Subscriptions – 1 year print & digital (4 issues): $79.95 within Australia incl. GST. Outside Australia $119.95. 2 years print & digital (8 issues): $149.95 within Australia incl. GST. 1 year digital only: $49.95.

Payment may be made by Mastercard or Visa, or by cheque made out to Schwartz Books. Payment includes postage and handling.

To subscribe, fill out and post the subscription form inside this issue, or subscribe online:

quarterlyessay.com
subscribe@blackincbooks.com
Phone: 61 3 9486 0288

Correspondence should be addressed to:

The Editor, Quarterly Essay
Level 1, 221 Drummond Street
Carlton VIC 3053 Australia
Phone: 61 3 9486 0288 / Fax: 61 3 9011 6106
Email: quarterlyessay@blackincbooks.com

Editor: Chris Feik. Management: Elisabeth Young. Publicity: Anna Lensky. Design: Guy Mirabella. Assistant Editor: Kirstie Innes-Will. Production Coordinator: Marilyn de Castro. Typesetting: Akiko Chan.

Printed in Australia by McPherson's Printing Group. The paper used to produce this book comes from wood grown in sustainable forests.

Map by Murray–Darling Basin Authority

LEGEND

- State borders
- Murray–Darling Basin
- Rivers/creeks
- Towns & cities
- Capital cities outside of MDB
- Major water storages
- Wetlands & natural lakes

CRY ME A RIVER

The Tragedy of the Murray–Darling Basin

Margaret Simons

I've come to think of the Murray–Darling Basin as being like a tree, except the sap runs not from root to twigs but in the other direction. The roots and trunk are in South Australia. Here the river runs pea-green between red cliffs through semi-desert country to the vast sheets of water that form the lower lakes, the Coorong and the sea. The main branches of the tree are the Murray itself, forming most of the border between New South Wales and Victoria, fed by the mighty Murrumbidgee and its tributaries and the rivers of Victoria. The other main branch is the Darling, or the Barwon–Darling, to give it both its northern and southern names. Its tributaries loop to the Great Dividing Range west of Sydney and splay into the braided floodplains of the tropics. The smaller branches and twigs spread across the inland, each one with a story, or many stories. Clancy of the Overflow, who worked on the Lachlan River before he went "to Queensland droving ... down the Cooper River, where the western drovers go." The Drover's Wife, who lived by a dried-up creek in the Henry Lawson story. It was probably a tributary of the Darling, although recent reimaginings relocate her to the Snowy Mountains. The European names of the rivers are gestures to the history of white nation-building – Lachlan, Macquarie, Darling, the Murray itself.

There are older stories. The Rainbow Serpent, which in the stories of the Barkandji lives in the waterholes of the Lower Darling, or the Barka as they prefer to call it. Or Ngurunderi, whose pursuit of Ponde – a Murray cod – created the channel of the Lower Murray.

You can give the figures – 77,000 kilometres of rivers, 2.6 million people, forty Aboriginal nations, 120 species of waterbirds – but they are abstractions from the reality.

It seems wrong that the word "basin" is so utilitarian, conjuring up images of kitchen implements and dishwater. This is a mighty thing. It covers more than a million square kilometres. One of the things that makes it hard to understand, to conceptualise, is its size. The water engineers call it one of the largest drainage areas in the world, which again makes one think of sinks and plugholes.

But it can also be thought of as a vast, cupped hand. This is how Badger Bates, a Barkandji elder, describes it. He was raised on the Barka and taught the traditional ways by his grandmother and extended family. He grew up to be a stockman and a park ranger. He says he never learnt to read and write properly, but today, at seventy-three, he carries himself with a natural authority that the bureaucrats and politicians struggling to govern the Basin can only envy. He stretches out his arm. "Here is my left hand, and in my palm the Barka starts. And here my fingers running to my palm are the Warrego, the Barwon, the Culgoa. Then here, my thumb joint, that is Wentworth, where the Barka meets the Murray. Then across where my left arm meets my shoulder, my body beyond" – he gestures to his chest, his skinny, hardened torso – "that is South Australia, right down to them lakes. And my right arm, here runs the Murray. So, our duty as Barkandji people is to fight for this river, to give them all water. We are connected."

But at the moment, and too many times in the last decade, the Darling doesn't run.

Water connects people, but it also divides. If politics is how human societies decide on the sharing of resources, wealth and power, then in a dry country water is indubitably, essentially and unavoidably political. The Basin and its water politics are in the news because of allegations of corruption and water theft, because of dead fish and angry irrigators, and because a royal commission in South Australia has suggested one of our important government organisations, the Murray–Darling Basin Authority, is dishonest, incompetent and acting outside the law. The narrative concerns the Murray–Darling Basin Plan and its implementation. To the management of the Murray–Darling we can attribute the rise of the Shooters, Fishers and Farmers Party, and an increasing atmosphere of panic – mixed with vaunting ambition – in the National Party, extending into the Coalition. And, most likely, Labor will not be able to win government unless it can address water politics, and with it one of the political fractures of our time: the divide and mutual incomprehension between those who earn their living directly from land and resources and those who don't.

There is a conventional, city-based view of rural Australia as locked in a time warp, unchanging and resistant to change. It is a dangerous and sentimental misunderstanding – as simplistic and out of touch as its rural-based counter, the view of city folk as soft-handed, soft-headed and divorced from hard realities. The speed of change for those who learn their living from the land outstrips anything city dwellers have dealt with in recent decades. Technology and mechanisation has devastated rural employment. New cropping methods – laser ploughing, preserving stubble on the soil – have had to be learnt, and in turn have kept more water in the soil. Free-market reforms have seen the death of the Australian Wheat Board and the other bodies that governed the production and marketing of agricultural products. Agricultural policy has been at once centralised and fragmented. Farmers have become futures traders, brokers in their own production. Agriculture and food production have been rapidly corporatised, from paddock to supermarket and container ship. In the 2015–16 Agricultural Census, there were about 86,000 farms in Australia. Ten years ago, there were 135,000.

This speed of change, and the stress and dislocation it causes, is the backdrop to water politics. Throughout the modern history of Australia, the Murray–Darling Basin has challenged our ability to operate as a nation. Now, it may bring politics as normal undone.

Since 2012, the Murray–Darling Basin Plan has sought to claw back the allocation of water to farmers in the area usually described as the food bowl of our nation (although, thanks to the increasing dominance of cotton, these days people prefer to talk of food and fibre). The Basin is Australia's most important agricultural region, producing around one-third of the national food supply, and a total of $24 billion in agricultural products. Australia is unusual in the world in that it can more than feed itself – producing more agricultural products than we can consume. That is thanks to the Basin. More than 3 million people rely on the river system for their drinking water. If you eat nuts or fruit or bread or meat or rice or vegetables, drink milk or wear cotton, then you are likely tangibly connected to the Murray–Darling.

But we are all in trouble. Over the latter part of the last century, it became clear that the river system was at breaking point. It could die. All that went with it – money, livelihoods, sense of nation – was at risk. There were many indicators, including salinity, blue-green algae, fish deaths and the closing of the Mouth. There were billabongs that smelt of rotten eggs. The Murray–Darling Basin Plan, devised over many years, is an attempt to solve that problem. It is the first attempt to manage the Basin as a whole, and to make its use sustainable. That means striking a different balance between water use and the environment, taking water back from farmers and using it to better manage the health of the river.

We are now at the halfway point of the Plan's twelve-year implementation and things seem to be falling apart. Meanwhile, people in the cities – and even those who live in the Basin – struggle to understand what the river system is and how it works. The water flows, usually, but the information doesn't. The water engineers of the Basin talk in terms of valleys – each river and each catchment. But the Basin is shallow, and these are not valleys in the European sense, each community divided from the other by hills and mountains. Rather, the people of the Basin are a society without being a community. A society in the sense that they live in an ordered, rule-bound way, the relationships between them governed. Not a community, because they struggle to recognise common interest.

In the Murray–Darling Basin, the authorities joke, everyone downstream is a wastrel, and everyone upstream is a thief. Only I, the person drawing water in this spot, for these crops, in this way, truly understands the value of the water and how to use it.

The Basin is a plumbed landscape – one of the most plumbed in the world. In the Southern Basin, it is tightly controlled. The Murrumbidgee and the Murray are reliable rivers, fed by snow melt in spring as well as by tributaries, and defined by big dams and storages – the Hume, the Dartmouth and others. Water is ordered up and delivered by rivers, pipes and channels to its end use. The Northern Basin is different. Here the rivers are boom and bust.

For water users, there is a welter of rules, different from state to state and valley to valley, governing exactly how the water is managed and shared. For all but the experts – and even for some of them – the rules are impenetrable. Taking a very broad brush to great complexity, one can own a licence to take water, and then an allocation is made against that licence, which varies depending on the season and the type of licence held. There are general security licences – the majority in the Basin – and high security licences, more likely to be held by the owners of crops, such as grapevines and fruit and nut trees, that remain in place for many harvests, needing water each year. There are also rules about "supplementary flows" – when the river is in flood or running high. Both licences to take water and allocations can be traded. Add to this that water users can in most places carry forward what they don't use, sometimes for as long as ten years, and that in some areas water is increasingly being stored in private dams, and it becomes hard to know why, for example, the farmer downstream or upstream or across the river is able to grow a crop when you are dry.

The Bureau of Meteorology gathers the information on water trading from the states, but publishes only at a macro level. Finding out how the system works in any particular area is almost impossible for an outsider. Attempts to penetrate the complexities of Basin management are not helped by the desiccated language of the bureaucracy, and of the water engineers who have, since before federation, dominated irrigation – the white man's dream of creating gardens in the desert. They speak of "events." That usually means that it has rained. A "major event" means that it has rained a lot. Sometimes an "event" means a release of water from a dam or storage. Then there are the key terms that underlie the Basin Plan, such as the sustainable diversion limit – a cap, in theory, on how much water can be extracted, which is then translated into caps for each area. This is not only dead language, but also confusing, even a lie, because the sustainable diversion limit is not sustainable, and may not be a limit. Academic critics of the Basin Plan have described water politics as having entered a "post-truth world."

Furthermore, the numbers are hard to grasp. The language of water management is megalitres and gigalitres – units most people can't visualise. A megalitre is 4 million cups of water, or a million one-litre milk bottles, or about 5000 baths. A gigalitre – the units in which the macro policy of the Basin is determined – is a billion litres, or a thousand megalitres. Sydney Harbour contains about 500 gigalitres. The average annual rainfall in the Murray–Darling Basin supplies about 508,000 gigalitres of fresh water, of which 94 per cent evaporates or transpires. In some seasons, more evaporates than falls as rain. About 2 per cent of the rain recharges groundwater aquifers. The remaining 4 per cent, or about 24,000 gigalitres, runs into streams and rivers. Another 1200 gigalitres or so is transferred from elsewhere, such as from the reliable waters of the Snowy River, diverted beneath the Great Dividing Range to the Murray and Murrumbidgee, making possible the rich green irrigation areas of Griffith and Leeton. Huge amounts are "lost," as the engineers say, to wetlands, evaporating or seeping into the soil – not really a loss, but a natural part of the river. Total water use by humans in the Basin, some from groundwater but mostly from the rivers, is 12,903 gigalitres a year, or about twenty-six Sydney Harbours. Most of that is for agriculture. About 5000 gigalitres flows to the sea.

But these are averages, and the large figures tell us little or nothing about any particular year, or any particular place. The Murray–Darling Basin Plan is macro policy, governed from Canberra. But it plays out in landscape that farmers and locals know with the intimacy of a lover.

Jody Swirepik is the Commonwealth Environmental Water Holder – the woman in charge of managing the water that has been clawed back for the environment under the Basin Plan. She describes a recent visit to the Lachlan River, where there was controversy over the release of 22 gigalitres of environmental water to flow down the length of the river, past drought-stricken properties to the Cumbung Swamp, the wetland at the junction of the Lachlan and the Murrumbidgee. The NSW Minister for Water, Melinda Pavey, said that the Water Holder was "pouring water down the river without any regard for our communities doing it tough." (In fact, the releases of water had been planned with the NSW government.)

I had been on the Lachlan a fortnight before Swirepik's visit. Irrigators told me they didn't understand what the Water Holder was trying to achieve. They worried an attempt was being made to maintain the swamp in a condition that could not be sustained, and that if the swamp "fell over" later, irrigators would cop the blame. Speaking in her office in Canberra, Swirepik reflected on how macro policy meets the realities of landscape: "The river is not a canal. It has all these complexities." For example, she had been told about a bank that used to be in the swamp – about a foot high for most of its length, which had held water back, creating a wetland and reedbeds. The locals told her that sometime in the last decade that little bank had been removed – nobody knew by whom. As a result, the wetland plants had disappeared. Did the Water Holder know about the removal of that little bank before her visit? Swirepik is sure some of her staff would have known. "But you have to get out into the landscape. There are so many stories of the river, you know, pub stories from twenty years ago, or people's recollection that there used to be a wetland here, and that they saw tens of thousands of birds breeding there and haven't seen that recently."

These stories of the river are increasingly contested, as the engineers attempt to model and restore some portion of "natural" flows. The irrigators on the Lachlan, in their interviews with me, posed the question of what the Water Holder thought the "natural" state of the Cumbung Swamp would have been, and what "sustainable" might look like. What is natural? What people remember from their childhood, what the traditional owners have recorded in stories, or what the water engineers' models tell us would once have happened before we built dams and locks and weirs and drew away so much of the water for our own use? And how to account for climate change? Swirepik comments: "The landscape has been changed over decades and sometimes we don't exactly know how … We are not trying to change things back to natural. That's not possible … We need to identify what areas of habitat and environmental values can be supported or restored." She agreed with the Lachlan River landholders that the Water Holder needed to work at the property level, to come to joint understandings of what can be sustained.

The natural state lies outside living memory, in the realm of dreaming and anecdote. In both the real and the political landscape of the Murray–Darling Basin, nature is often referred to, used as a justification for action, but increasingly it is out of reach, a concept rather than a reality.

Some of the stories of the river are well known and can be read on signposts at tourist spots. Some of them are buried or disputed. Parts of the landscape speak loud. Some speak soft, and some have lost their stories entirely.

*

The Murray–Darling Basin Plan is at once a water management plan, an ecologically driven document and a political compact, all embedded in narratives of land and water. One of my aims in this essay is to rescue those narratives from the abstract, explain the Plan and the system it is trying to govern, and explore why things seem to be falling apart. At the heart of the narrative is the collision between the realities of the landscape – the intimate details, the banks and tributaries, the complexities of community and society – and macro policy, the affairs of the nation.

I did a lot of driving – all over the Basin. Rural Australia no longer lies at the heart of our national narrative, but as I travelled snatches of poetry came to me. The sunlit plain extended. The drover's life has pleasures city folk never know. A land of drought and flooding rains. Its beauty and its terror. In the lower lakes, sun played on sheets of water, and I could smell the sea and hear the roar of breakers on the beach beyond the dunes. On moonlit nights I fancied I could understand why so many stories of the Ngarrindjeri tell of people travelling from the lake country to the sky.

Around Loxton in the South Australian Riverland, and over the border near Mildura, I saw hectares and hectares of new plantings – mostly almond trees, catering to the trend for almond milk, driven in part by concern about the impact of dairy cattle on a warming planet. Alongside the almond trees were abandoned grapevines, bulldozed into piles or left to stand like skeletons, fingers pointing to the sky, and in between red dust – a reminder that, without water, this is desert.

I drove across the Hay Plains, so flat I could detect the curvature of the earth. The road trains swam towards me through water mirages. There were curtains of rain when I was there, and the overpowering smell of water on dry. The land glowed orange. So did the low walls of newly constructed private dams, springing up on land never previously irrigated.

On the road from Wilcannia to Broken Hill there were willy-willies all over the plain, the columns of red dust rising to the sky like pillars in the vast hall of the inland.

Drought is an abstract word when spoken in the city – defined by figures of rainfall, or "events." But around Dubbo and Narromine, it became real.

The sky was dirty-brown because of the dust. The paddocks looked as though they had been targeted by a vast vacuum cleaner. I stopped in the tiny, evocatively named town of Nevertire, on the edge of the saltbush country that extends west to the deserts of the interior, and my car was buffeted by the big road trains carrying fodder to cattle inland. Not far away was the Auscott cotton gin factory. No cotton was being grown there, because there was no water, but the ash-coloured waste from the last crop was bundled in the paddocks, and fur balls of white were strewn by the side of the road – baubles on khaki.

Further north, pursuing the Darling to its headwaters, I drove the road between Dirranbandi and St George. In drought, wildlife comes to the roads, because tiny run-offs of condensation or rain allow vegetation to survive on the verge. That means roadkill. For some reason this road was particularly bad. It was like driving through an abattoir or a deli counter. Raw meat, dried meat, fermented meat and the constant crunch of bone.

Further east, as I approached the rim of the Basin and the Darling Ranges, even the prickly pear – that introduced scourge of the inland, which once made 40,000 square kilometres of farming land unproductive – was wilting. The spiky pads were wrinkled and pointing to the ground.

It was a big journey and my companions included pride, fear, horror and awe. Sentimental, perhaps, but often I had a lump in my throat and tears in my eyes. The beauty and the terror. The vastness of the Basin, and the wonder and the awfulness of our attempts to manage it.

THE PLAN

The Garden of Eden was irrigated, according to the great holy books that emerged from the Middle East. The word "Eden" derives from Aramaic root words that mean fruitful and well-watered. The idea of gardens in the desert – and the politics of water scarcity – are as old as civilisation. Australia's water users might reflect on the fact that the word "rival," now meaning adversary, was originally used in Roman law to mean those who shared the water of a *rivus*, or irrigation channel.

Mike Young is a professor at the University of Adelaide's Centre for Global Food and Resources. He is also one of the architects of Australia's system of water trading, generally acknowledged as one of the most advanced in the world. He regularly advised the then water minister Malcolm Turnbull when the *Water Act 2007*, which established the Murray–Darling Basin Plan and the Murray–Darling Basin Authority, was being devised. Young didn't win all his battles – about which more later – but he says today that the system underlying the Plan is close to world's best practice. But despite that, he says, the design is flawed and the execution lacking.

Young recounts the history of irrigation, taking evident pleasure in the contemporary comparisons. The first people to deal with water scarcity and irrigation were in Mesopotamia. "They made tunnels to go up into the mountains, and ran the water out to villages in the deserts." People were allocated shares in the system. A share record book was kept in each village, and water was tradeable. Every fortnight or so, the village administration would sell enough water to pay the wage of the water master. The system was so successful it spread across northern Africa and into Spain, and from there to the colonies of the Americas. Alfred Deakin, who was to become Australia's second prime minister, led a visit to California in 1884 and persuaded the Chaffey brothers, irrigation entrepreneurs, to come to Australia. They founded the irrigation settlements of Mildura and Renmark. Deakin introduced the first laws to promote irrigation, placing the ownership of water with the Crown, and allowing for the establishment of state-aided irrigation works by local trusts and cooperatives.

The water of the Murray–Darling system was one of the most bitterly contested issues when the founding fathers met in the 1890s to argue over the constitution. The debates were full of insult, rhetoric about armed conflict and threats to pull out of discussions, derailing federation. The result was Section 100 of the constitution, which reads: "The Commonwealth shall not, by any law or regulation of trade or commerce, abridge the right of a State or of the residents therein to the reasonable use of the waters of rivers for conservation or irrigation." In simple terms, the states own and manage the water. The Commonwealth has power only so far as the states agree. But this was only a partial settlement. The issue of how to deal with the competing rights of each state was never settled, with the founding fathers anticipating it would be for the High Court to determine. In fact, the High Court has never had to consider such a case. That time may be coming.

The states managed their differences through intergovernmental agreements, beginning with the River Murray Waters Agreement in 1915, up to the present-day and the Murray–Darling Basin Agreement, which led to the Plan. Under these agreements, inflows upstream of Albury and the giant Hume Dam are shared half and half between New South Wales and Victoria. Downstream of Albury, each state owns the water from its own tributaries, including the Murrumbidgee in New South Wales and the Ovens, Goulburn, Campaspe and Loddon rivers in Victoria. As for the Darling River, the sharing of water depends on inflows to the Menindee Lakes. If the lakes fall below a certain level, New South Wales manages the water to supply the towns of the Lower Darling and, until recently, Broken Hill. Over a certain level, the water is managed by the Murray–Darling Basin Authority and shared equally between Victoria and New South Wales. Finally, South Australia gets a more or less guaranteed annual share: 1850 gigalitres. This is supplied equally by New South Wales and Victoria. From this, South Australia supplies irrigators, water to Adelaide and rural towns, and operates the river, including running water out to the sea, flushing the salt. Queensland was a latecomer to irrigation, with the industry getting off the ground only from the 1970s – but growing fast around the tight-knit cotton industry.

The Tasmanian Dam Case in the High Court, in 1983 during the Hawke government, laid the foundation for a shift in the power relationships. The High Court found that the Commonwealth could use its external affairs power to give effect to international treaties, particularly those concerning the environment. This narrow window of contested Commonwealth power, together with a large dose of fragile political compact, is the eye of the needle through which the behemoth of the Murray–Darling Basin Plan has so far managed to squeeze.

In 1987, with Labor governments in power in South Australia, New South Wales, Victoria and the Commonwealth, the Basin states met to formalise what became the Murray–Darling Basin Agreement, with a ministerial council including the water ministers from each Basin state and territory, and the Commonwealth. It was already clear, from the regularity with which the Murray Mouth closed, from the quality of the water and the condition of the wetlands, that more water was being taken from the system than could be sustained, but little progress was made on reducing it. History suggests that it is only when there is a visible crisis that progress is made on managing the river. In the early 1990s, that crisis was a toxic blue-green algae bloom infecting more than 1000 kilometres. The shock of the water turning poison made clear to everyone that the water had been drastically over-allocated and that action had to be taken to save the river system and all it supported. The Murray–Darling Basin Commission was set up. A few years later, in 1995, a cap was put on allocations, although it was not fully imposed and was constantly disputed between the states.

Underlying this process were reforms – of a piece with the free-market enthusiasm of the 1980s and '90s. Originally, water licences were attached to particular pieces of land. Starting in 1994, they were progressively unbundled, and trade encouraged. You could own land and sell the water licence that had belonged to it. Or you could own water without owning land. The idea was that if water could be traded, the market would ensure it found its highest-value use.

The implications of this policy are still unwinding. It is one of the reasons hectares of almonds have been planted near the border. The companies concerned have deep pockets and can fight it out on the water market to make sure their trees will stay alive. But in a drought, the prices rise.

*

The turn of the century brought the next crisis: the millennium drought. In 2004, the Howard government began a program unique in the world, in that it allowed for a formal return of water to the river system for environmental purposes. A new piece of legislation, the *Water Act*, was devised in a crashing hurry, caused both by the desire to capitalise on the crisis with real reform and by the fact that the government expected to lose the impending 2007 election. The act, steered through by Turnbull, passed in the dying days of the Howard government. It established the Murray–Darling Basin Authority in place of the pre-existing commission, and also the office of the Commonwealth Environmental Water Holder, to manage water recovered for the environment. It was a pivot in the history of the river – a landmark piece of legislation – but the ownership of water, under the constitution, remained with the states. The Howard government asked the states to refer their powers to the Commonwealth. Victoria, under the Bracks Labor government, refused.

Howard pressed ahead regardless. He remarked in mid-2007 that while the constitution gave the Commonwealth sufficient powers to force reform in the Basin, they were not sufficient to ensure an ideal scheme. The *Water Act* relied for its constitutional validity on an international treaty, the Ramsar Convention on Wetlands, which takes its name from the small Iranian town where it was signed in 1971. The Ramsar Convention obliges governments to manage and conserve designated wetlands, sixteen of which are in the Murray–Darling Basin.

The *Water Act* was attempting to achieve environmental, social and economic aims, but because of the constitutional issue it had to be framed primarily as a piece of environmental legislation, with social and economic aims tacked on. So while its principal aim was to return water extraction to environmentally sustainable levels, and to "protect, restore and provide for the ecological values of ecosystems," it also talked about promoting "economic, social and environmental outcomes." The conflict between those words was the basis for a finding by the recent South Australian royal commission that the Authority had acted illegally, and unconstitutionally, in trying for a "triple bottom line" approach, putting economic and social issues on an equal footing with the environment.

Mike Young believes that Turnbull intended to establish the equivalent of a Reserve Bank for water – free of political control, or at least from the control of the states. That attempt failed. The states fought back. After the election of the Rudd government, the new minister for climate change and water, Penny Wong, was forced to give the ministerial council more power. The politicians remained in control.

By the time Rudd came to power, the river redgums along the sides of the river were dying. Water allocations were cut everywhere. There were fears in many states that the big cities would run out of drinking water. State governments planned desalination plants, cotton production fell away completely, and Australia began to import most of its rice.

The main initial task of the Murray–Darling Basin Authority was to use the "best available science" to devise a Basin plan, incorporating every aquifer and irrigation channel. It was to be the first-ever comprehensive audit, and it was meant to reveal how much water was being taken and could be taken on a sustainable basis. This was to lead to a new figure: the sustainable diversion limit, or SDL, both for the Basin as a whole and translated to each catchment and valley. It was a massive research undertaking, with huge economic implications. Clearly, there would be reductions in water allocation as the balance between use and environment was struck anew. Livelihoods would be affected, futures compromised and townships hit. Throughout the Rudd government, as it wrestled with the high-profile complexities of climate change, the compilation of the Plan bubbled away, a potent but sleeping political issue – keenly appreciated in Basin communities, but largely neglected and not understood by city-based media and many politicians. The draft Murray–Darling Basin Plan was due to be released in 2010.

In the meantime, Wong moved fast to recover water, not waiting for the Plan. Howard had set aside $10 billion to address over-allocation. Labor promised to bring forward some of that to start buying water from farmers for return to the environment. Wong saw it as an opportunity. Farmers were desperate after the drought, and many were willing to sell. Wong says today she always assumed that the millennium drought was not just a drought – that, thanks to climate change, there would be even less water in the years ahead. The process moved quickly, with little investigation of the economic impact on rural communities. This period is remembered throughout the Basin. They call it the time of "Pennies from Heaven." Many irrigators sold their water to the Commonwealth – sometimes all of it, usually only part. People were on their knees, heavily in debt from the drought.

Meanwhile, the states had yet to agree to refer their water powers to the Commonwealth. Wong and Rudd cut a deal. It was a hard piece of pragmatic politics, but it broke the deadlock. The crucial factor was the Commonwealth chequebook. Victoria was brought on board with a $1 billion sweetener – journalists wrote it up as a bribe – in funding for the "Food-Bowl Modernisation Project," one of the first of the much-vaunted "efficiency projects" that remain controversial. It was the beginning of constant spending by the Commonwealth on efficiency programs – millions of dollars handed out to individual farmers and communities, some of it justified, much of it a political fix.

After the October 2010 election, Labor entered minority government, dependent on the support of two rural independents, including the member for New England, Tony Windsor. Two months later, the Guide to the proposed Murray–Darling Basin Plan was released. The research had been done in a hurry, but was internationally peer-reviewed, scientifically based, open and transparent. It was clear when it was compiled that not enough was known about the Northern Basin, in particular its boom and bust rivers. Hence a review of the Northern Basin was planned. The ranges that had been considered for the all-important SDLs, the caps on use, were large, the political implications huge. But the *Water Act* said politics should not come into it. The SDLs should be based on the "best available science." So it was that the Guide suggested cuts of between 27 and 37 per cent of the water drawn for irrigation, with some rivers targeted for cuts of up to 45 per cent. This would return an extra 3000 to 4000 gigalitres of water to the environment – said to be enough to ensure that the Murray Mouth would be open nearly all the time: a key indicator of the health of the system, given the need to flush salt to the sea.

The Guide – over a thousand pages of technical information – was released on a Friday, and the following Monday consultations began. For rural communities, the figures were astonishing, and apparently unexpected. It is hard, from the city and a distance of ten years, to recreate the emotion. Big men cried. There were orchestrated burnings of the document among signs asking "Is Hitler reborn?" The president of the Victorian Farmers Federation described the document as proposing a "legislated drought." Suicides were attributed to the release of the Guide.

Windsor was horrified, and made water politics part of the deal under which Gillard was able to form minority government. He chaired a new Standing Committee on Regional Australia. It considered the Guide and was scathing. It recommended a complete rethink, a halt to "non-strategic" water buybacks and more investment in community-driven water efficiency projects. Today, the Windsor report is largely forgotten in the Basin – which is surprising, because many of the things it recommended have come to pass.

Not only were the irrigation communities ill-prepared for the release of the Guide, but the Gillard government apparently had no strategy to deal with the political consequences – other than to crumble. Tony Burke had replaced Penny Wong as water minister. The Windsor inquiry was underway. Amid all the pressure, Burke – and the Murray–Darling Basin Authority itself – backed away from the Plan and began to demonstrate a willingness to compromise on what the detailed scientific data suggested was needed. Burke told parliament that he had sought legal advice from the Australian Government Solicitor on the meaning of the *Water Act* and that advice supported taking account of economic and social factors in decision-making.

Bret Walker SC, the head of the South Australian royal commission, has since described this advice as "dubious" and said it drew "incorrect conclusions," but the Authority and successive governments have relied on it ever since. The argument goes that the amount of water that can be taken from the river on a sustainable basis is necessarily within a range, and in deciding on a figure within that range "there is scope to consider social and economic factors, to optimise an outcome."

Armed with the legal advice, Labor began attempting a political fix. The then chair of the Authority, Mike Taylor, resigned in December 2010 because he was under pressure from Burke to compromise the environmental needs for social and economic objectives. Taylor was replaced by a former NSW planning minister, Craig Knowles, who continued the back-pedalling and became actively hostile to the Guide. It was, Knowles said, time to move on from the figures it had suggested.

Within a year, the Basin Guide was treated by everyone as irrelevant. By April 2011, a process of negotiation had begun around a new, much lower amount to be recovered for the environment.

David Pearce is the principal of the Centre for International Economics, a private research agency. His group was brought in by the Authority and charged with attempting a cost–benefit analysis of the Basin Plan. It was a difficult undertaking – which became more so. The figures on agricultural production were well known and comparatively robust. But how to put a figure on the value of the environment? His team drew on a range of studies that had asked people how they valued native fish, waterbirds or other aspects of the natural world in order to work out how much they would be prepared to pay per kilometre of river improved. One study suggested that the average household was prepared to pay about 20 cents a year for a healthy river system.

When Pearce and his team began, they were working on the basis of 3500 gigalitres for environmental uses – the figure in the now much-criticised Guide. But as the work proceeded, he was told it was going to be lower. "I had no insight into why." One now-retired Authority staff member heard jokes about the recovery target being linked to a NSW postcode: "everyone understood the figure had to start with a 2." Pearce's "intuitive sense" in talking to the ecologists was that this change would not provide enough water "to do what you needed to do for the ecology." That, too, was the consensus of those who gave evidence to the South Australian royal commission. An SDL derived from a water-recovering target beginning with 2 would not be sustainable at all, they said

Pearce and his team continued to struggle with the cost–benefit analysis. Nothing about it was simple, and there were huge uncertainties. "The Murray–Darling is a complex system. Put in more water, and there isn't necessarily a linear response, but my sense was that if you had more gigalitres available for the environment then you had a better chance of controlling all of the aspects of the flow regime that the system needs," he recalls.

After discussions with the Authority, Pearce had agreed not to follow his usual practice and include a table putting benefits and costs side by side. There were two reasons. First, the enormous level of uncertainty. Second were the "communications difficulties, shall we say, with farmers in Griffith and so on." The Authority was nervous. The question was, "How can we communicate this without making it too obvious that there are areas where the costs are bigger than the benefits, and also areas where the benefits are bigger than the costs?" In other words, there would be winners and losers. Pearce comments:

> Even if you had perfect politics and perfect administration of the Basin, there could still be mistakes and things could still go wrong, because it's just so complex. In the long run, I think all they can do is experiment. Of course you should keep funding the scientists to do the research and fund various models, but you also need to have some large-scale experiments to understand what happens, and then to adjust accordingly.

But how do you tell people that it is necessary to experiment upon them, on their self-image and on their livelihood?

In 2012, Labor finally legislated the Basin Plan, with an amount to be returned to the environment of 2750 gigalitres a year. None of the scientists who have reviewed the figure regard it as consistent with the evidence of what was needed, even if the likely impact of climate change is ignored. The Wentworth Group of Concerned Scientists, an independent action committee, described it as "[manipulating] science in an attempt to engineer a pre-determined political outcome," and few disagree. But if it hadn't been done, would the Plan have been created at all?

It wasn't the end of the political fixes. Labor lost power in September 2013, and the implementation of the Plan fell to the incoming Abbott government. Partly because of the record of that implementation, in early 2018 the Labor government in South Australia, led by Jay Weatherill, set up its royal commission into the Murray–Darling Basin Plan, in the face of opposition from the Commonwealth government and most of the states. Two months after setting up the commission, the Weatherill government lost power.

The commission gave everyone involved a terrible pasting. The story of the Basin Plan, said Walker, was "a story of cynical disregard ... to the lasting discredit of all those who manipulated the processes to this end." He expressed his "admiring praise" for the *Water Act*, for its setting into legislation an environmental aim, informed by science. So too, with reservations, for the making of the Plan and its achievement in getting the states to cooperate. But, he said, there was "deep pessimism" about whether the aims could be achieved. "There are many ways in which study of the grand national endeavour in question leaves a decidedly sour taste." The Authority, he said, had been dishonest and guilty of obfuscation and maladministration, willing to massage the science for political purposes. Walker did not recommend that South Australia should sue the Commonwealth or the other states, but his findings clearly left open the possibility of future litigation, including High Court challenges.

Walker's report made headlines, but the upstream states were quick to dismiss it as a piece of political positioning by the former Weatherill government. The consensus among governments and bureaucrats was that the Plan is too important, and the political compact behind it too fragile, to entertain a wholesale review of its wisdom and validity. The new South Australian state government also disowned many of the commission's findings.

Since then, as we shall see, the politics have become close to unmanageable. New South Wales is threatening to withdraw from the Plan – and is in any case refusing to implement key parts. There has been a constant sprouting of inquiries and reviews into water matters by different bodies, federal and state. Some of them have been an attempt to keep the show on the road in the face of political tensions and evidence of maladministration.

In 2017, Barnaby Joyce was replaced as water minister by the National Party's David Littleproud. who spent most of his time in the portfolio trying to hold things together in the wake of what even National Party insiders describe as a "wild ride" during Joyce's time. A new inquiry or review seems to be proposed every time the Plan is challenged or threatens to fall apart. It's a high-wire performance of political management – review, inquiry and adjustment, but never the risky business of questioning the fundamentals.

The Australian Competition and Consumer Commission is inquiring into the fairness of the market for water, and allegations of water hoarding by commodities traders. As well, in late 2019 Littleproud set up an independent panel to "assess social and economic conditions impacting communities across the Murray–Darling Basin." The Australian National Audit Office is looking into water-buying by the Commonwealth during Joyce's time as minister. Lastly, the grandly titled but effectively impotent Interim Inspector-General of Murray–Darling Basin Water Resources, Mick Keelty, is also inquiring into Basin matters – about which more later. There is also an ongoing Productivity Commission review of the Plan. And the NSW Independent Commission Against Corruption is investigating allegations of corruption and water theft, first raised by *Four Corners* in 2017.

While I was touring the Basin, some of these inquiries were often a day ahead of me or on my tail. At their community consultations, they heard litanies of distress and complaint in which water politics were mixed up with all the other issues in fast-changing rural Australia – the shrinking of communities, the reform weariness, the existential angst of the move away from the heart of the national narrative, the feeling that even though these inquiries were there to listen, the voices of rural people would never be properly heard.

*

You can hear crazy talk in the Murray–Darling Basin. I met people who spoke of terrorism. There were suggestions that farmers "who know how to use explosives" would blow up the barrages that divide the lower lakes in South Australia from the sea, because the evaporation from the lower lakes was robbing the system of water. I wondered, as I travelled, if ASIO and the Department of Home Affairs were across this? Were undercover security agents also travelling alongside, behind and ahead of me, tapping into the heated talk on social media and watching the sale of explosives – and the places where farmers gather?

When I challenged them, these farmers were quick to downgrade their threats to peaceful demonstration – perhaps accompanied by a little vandalism. They said they would take their cue from the inner-city climate emergency and Extinction Rebellion protesters. If *they* could bring cities to a halt, why not farmers? The Australian Citizens' Party, a minor far-right political party, has put out material suggesting the Basin Plan is an international conspiracy, led by former Goldman Sachs Australia boss and water minister Malcolm Turnbull, to loot Australia.

There are other wild rumours. As the price of water skyrockets, a commonly heard allegation is that Eddie McGuire and either former water minister Penny Wong or her Malaysian businessman father own huge amounts of water and are responsible for hoarding it, waiting for the drought to push prices up. McGuire has ridiculed the suggestion on his radio program. There is no truth in it at all, he said. The allegation is more serious against Wong, given she is a former water minister and instigator of the buybacks. She says the proposition is:

> completely untrue. These suggestions are so wrong that I would call them ridiculous, except I take seriously the deep anxiety that has enabled these ideas to flourish. Clearly people have don't confidence in the water market, and how could they when there is no transparency over who owns what? ... People have a right and a need to know who owns the water in the Basin and I support whatever is required to enable that.

Wong is right – conspiracy theories are fed by a lack of transparency. While it is possible to find out who owns shares in an Australian company, or who owns real estate, it is not possible for the ordinary citizen to find out who owns water, either in the system as a whole or in a particular catchment. You have to know the number of the relevant licence, and there is no searchable central list of such licences.

It would be wrong to suggest most, or even a reasonable minority, of farmers subscribe to crazy talk. But the rural communities of the Basin are labouring under a great weight of reform fatigue. Farmers have, for decades now, spent many hours driving to meetings at which they are consulted – or at least told about what is going to happen. They can't afford to miss the meetings, or they will certainly be ignored. It is a vast, mostly unpaid and unfunded effort, fuelled by self-interest, to be sure, but also public-spirited. This is the counter to the crazy talk of the disaffected. Farmers' involvement in water reform amounts to an ongoing participation in governance, taking place across the Basin, invisible or misunderstood from the cities.

The conspiracy theories are a backdrop to a pervasive lack of trust in governments of all complexions – a situation summarised by the chair of South Australian Murray Irrigators, Caren Martin, as "state hating on state, crops hating on crops, upstream hating on downstream, downstream hating on upstream." This is a society, but not a community.

The story of the Murray–Darling Basin, and the Plan that is our modern attempt to manage it, is a story of our nation, the things that join and divide us. It asks whether our current systems – our society and its communities – can possibly meet the needs of the nation and the certainty of change. Is the Plan an honest compact, and is it fair? Can it work? Are our politics up to the task? And what happens when the abstracts, the macro policy, the plumbing, the schemes, the "events" or the lack of them hit the realities of the landscape and the figures within it?

There are many stories in the answer to those questions. You could start telling them from the headwaters, or from the Mouth. I chose the middle, one of the saddest places in Australia.

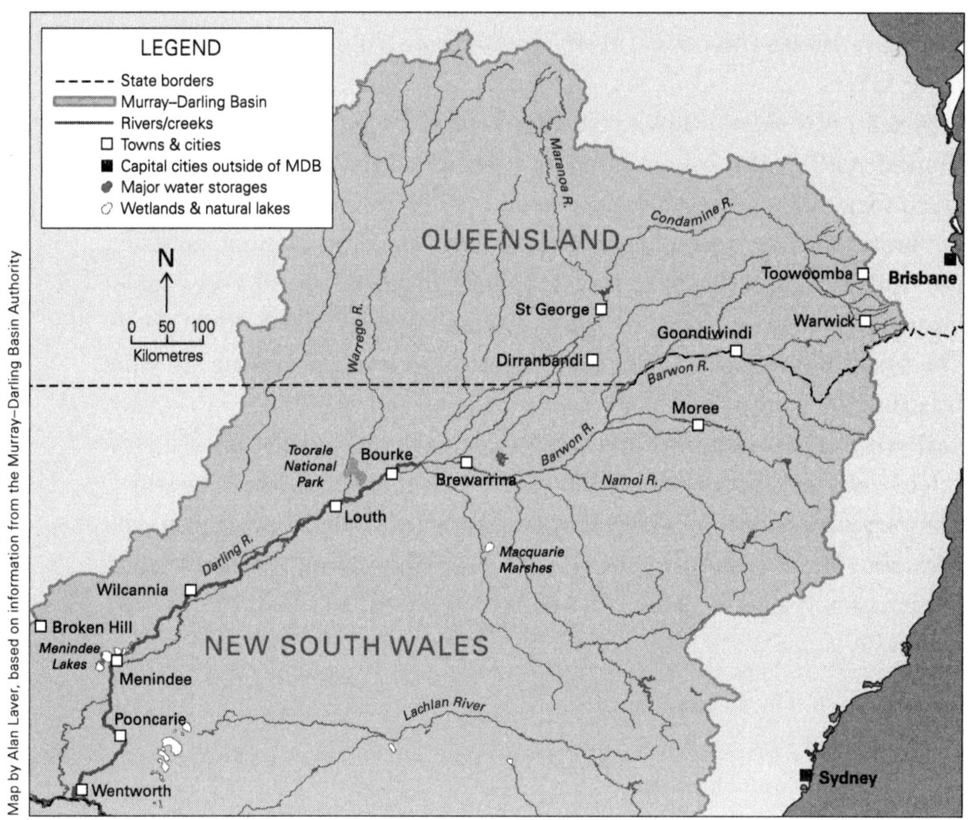

Map by Alan Laver, based on information from the Murray–Darling Basin Authority

The Old Wharf Café in Pooncarie is a fishing shed repurposed by its owners to serve the grey nomads who, in a good season, brave the bull-dust roads and the saltbush plains to see the mighty Darling River. Here, you can buy the Big Breakfast – sausages, beans, black pudding, eggs and more – and sit facing the old wharf, which was, back in the 1800s, a staging place for the river steamers heading upstream to Menindee and Wilcannia and downstream to Mildura. There is an old gum tree that has seen it all – the first white men, and probably a few generations of Barkandji before that. Burke and Wills camped near here for two weeks. There are the Indigenous stories too – of the Pooncarie mission and the women who travelled up and down this river with their children to prevent them being taken.

When I was there – a clear blue day in mid-December – the landscape showed itself in the colours used by its mapmakers, as though they had taken their palette direct from the land – pastel greys and pinks, washed-out browns, white trees and grey dust. Before breakfast, I scrambled down the bank to look at the river. It wasn't there. Instead, I found a few ankle-deep puddles. Some, in a break from the pastel palette, were a bright green. The trees on either side of the banks seemed to lean in, looking for what was absent.

If you tell the owners of the Old Wharf Café you are a journalist, you might get a discount. The people of the Lower Darling like journalists. They want more of them. The café plays songs by a local, Tony Smith, who now runs the Wentworth Caravan Park. He sings about that old tree on the wharf and all it has seen. And then comes a ballad called "The Dying Darling."

> What lies in the shallows
> Where I have just been?
> Dead fish and blue algae
> Still water gone green

But the words that stayed with me are in the chorus, mournful and pleading:

> Won't someone please take me
> Where I can be heard?
> The Darling is dying.
> Please take my word.

Viewed on Google Earth, the towns of the Lower Darling – Pooncarie, Menindee and Wilcannia – are specks on 300 kilometres of the river channel, running through red and grey dirt and mauve saltbush. These are tiny towns. Pooncarie had a population of 166 in the 2016 census, Menindee 551. Wilcannia, population of 549, is around 80 per cent Aboriginal. No elections turn on these votes and, until very recently, visits by politicians and journalists were almost unheard of.

This area, in particular the Menindee Lakes, is central to the story of the Murray–Darling Basin Plan. But that story could easily have played out with nobody other than the locals and the water bureaucrats noticing, were it not for what happened in the summer of 2018 and 2019, when a new colour was added to the pastels in the landscape: the silver of millions of fish bellies, turned upwards to the sun.

The Darling has always been a river of extremes. Unlike the Murrumbidgee and the Murray, it doesn't have the reliable boost of snow melt in spring. Rather, it draws from the boom-and-bust rains of the semi-tropical north. But in recent years, the river has moved past natural variability and towards death. Since the 1980s, when the cotton industry began to expand up north, flows to the Menindee Lakes have been reducing. More recently, there is evidence that the way water has been managed upstream has pushed the Lower Darling into drought up to three years earlier than the river upstream – a dirty, sad story. A constellation of rapid changes leads locals to the conclusion that in its quest to keep more powerful irrigation communities happy, the NSW government, with the complicity of the Commonwealth, has effectively decided to sacrifice the Lower Darling. In the words of the water engineers, the Darling is increasingly often not part of the "connected system" – meaning it no longer runs and no longer contributes water to the Murray. Since 2004, there have been four long periods when the Darling has ceased to flow. The present period is the longest since records began.

The impact on the locals is hard to adequately describe. Cindy Bates, CEO of the Menindee Aboriginal land council, says when there is no river for fishing and swimming, when there are signs up in town warning people to stay away from the water for fear of toxic blue-green algae, the Barkandji begin to die. In Wilcannia, crime rates correlate with the presence or absence of water. The towns of the Lower Darling ran out of water long ago – before towns running out of water became a commonplace national news story. The local council has dug bores, and water in boxes is trucked in. At great speed, the NSW government built a pipeline from Wentworth to Broken Hill to provide that city's water, which previously came from the Menindee Lakes.

Earlier, in 2014 – two years after the Basin Plan was legislated – six family farms – supporting ten families – between Menindee and Wentworth were told that it would no longer be possible to guarantee them a reliable water supply, due to planned changes in management of the Menindee Lakes. They should wind up their highly productive and profitable businesses, tear up their trees and vines, junk their irrigation pipes and seek compensation. Rachel Strachan and Alan Whyte are two of those farmers. Strachan's house looks over the Darling between Wentworth and Pooncarie. In a wet year, she can hitch a boat to her veranda post. When she spoke to me there, in mid-December, the river was a puddle far below us. There have been fewer and fewer wet years. Whyte and Strachan are not poor people. Their businesses have been profitable for generations. They are negotiating hard-to-get compensation that reflects that worth. But in the meantime, they are seeing a whole way of life come to an end – businesses built up and laboured over becoming piles of junk. According to Strachan, "We have good days and bad days."

Whyte showed me around his property – trees had been ripped up, others were dying and the poly irrigation pipe was coiled into piles destined for the dump. But there were some trees that were clearly being watered. He showed me a stretch of the Darling, and was almost shamefaced as we approached. "What I am about to show you, none of us are arguing is a solution. It's kind of an awful thing. An abomination." There, spanning the river from bank to bank, was an earth bank, entirely blocking the riverbed.

It was holding back a small pool of water. It's hard to describe the impact of seeing this crude earth bank. It is such a pedestrian thing – a makeshift dam – yet also profoundly shocking. It says this is no longer a river.

This bank – one of four – was built at the expense of the NSW taxpayer to hold back a tiny amount of remaining water and give Whyte and the other five farms one more crop, as well as providing nearby grazing properties with water for stock. When the river runs once more, it will be torn down – again at taxpayer expense. Whyte keeps a record of the depth of the pool with a marker pen on two old doors propped against a tree. There is a meter as well, but he prefers his own bush method. Regardless, the pool is now almost empty, and the families here can't bathe or wash in water drawn from it without getting a rash. Whyte sees the construction of these banks by the NSW government as a tacit admission of unfairness – that he, his neighbours and one of Australia's most storied rivers are the sacrifices on the altar of the Murray–Darling Basin Plan and the need to claw back water while avoiding the wrath of more politically connected water users upstream, in cotton country.

But the decline in flows to the Lower Darling started years before the current drought. Two stories – of the Barwon–Darling Water Resource Plan, and the management of the Menindee Lakes – put this region at the heart of the narrative of the Murray–Darling Basin Plan and its problems.

*

The tin tacks of the Basin Plan are the water resource plans devised by the states, area by area, valley by valley. Once devised, they are assessed by the Authority and, all being well, accredited by the Commonwealth water minister. There were to be thirty-three of them altogether, twenty in New South Wales. In the lead-up to the Plan, it was agreed that existing water resource plans would apply until new arrangements were in place.

The water rescue plan for the Barwon–Darling – the river upstream of Bourke – had been under negotiation for nearly eight years. After a long process, it went on public display for eighteen months, and submissions were made and received. A settlement was reached in June 2012. Then, at the last minute, and without most people knowing it was being done, the NSW minister responsible for water, Katrina Hodgkinson, yielded to lobbying by a Bourke-based cotton-industry lobbyist, Ian Cole, and everything changed. Cole is a powerful man. At that time, he owned Darling Farms, which he later sold to the nut grower Websters. Cole also owned the Bourke local paper and the radio station. Cole, you will hear in cotton country, is a man who knows how to get his way.

In the north of the Basin, the right to pump water often relies on the level of the river. Above a certain level, the pumps can be turned on. Cole had written directly to the minister on 14 May 2012 and again on 31 July, pressing his case. The essence of the changes Cole got through was that the irrigators upstream of Bourke would be allowed to start pumping earlier, intercepting lower flows.

When the parliament passed the Murray–Darling Basin Plan in November 2012, the unscrutinised water resource plan was adopted and remains in place today. It was, as Whyte says, a piece of bastardry, and it took some time for the farmers downstream of Bourke to realise what had happened.

Whyte and Strachan said they realised they were no longer receiving what they call "low flows." As Whyte puts it, when there is plenty of water, everyone is happy. They can tie up boats to their veranda posts and watch waters roll downstream – plenty for everyone. But between the booms, the continuing health of the river depends on the smaller rain "events" and the resulting low flows. Since 2012, those low flows have been largely intercepted.

The Basin Authority's chief executive, Phillip Glyde, admits that the Authority didn't realise the significance of what had happened until it was too late. He wasn't in the job then, but says: "I think the sentiment from the people who were here at the time is that they weren't made aware of the extent of the change and the consequences of those changes. There had been eight years of consultations on the Barwon–Darling Water Resource Plan, but all that was brushed aside."

Here is the gap between macro policy in Canberra and the realities on the ground. Here is the reality of lack of Commonwealth power. Glyde says: "Even now I don't think that anyone in the Commonwealth, or indeed the Murray–Darling Basin Authority, could say they had a detailed knowledge of the individual operation of every single rule in every single valley in the Plan." Even if the Authority had picked up on the significance of the changes, it is doubtful they could have done anything about it. Managing water is the business of the states.

The consequences were enormous. The NSW Natural Resources Commission, in a report released in September 2019, declared that the changes to the Barwon Darling water-sharing plan meant that low flows critical to the environment had been diverted. "The provisions benefit the economic interests of a few upstream users over the ecological and social needs of the many." There was "clear evidence" that this had caused "more frequent and longer cease to flow periods." The late changes to the water resource plan are now among the matters being investigated by the NSW ICAC. And, in September 2019, the NSW government proposed a new plan for the Barwon–Darling that would prevent the taking of water when the river is extremely low. Submissions were invited, but at the time of writing, no decision has been made – and nor have the submissions been made public.

For the Barkandji, there is a particularly painful irony in this story. In June 2015, after eighteen years of fighting, they succeeded in being recognised as traditional owners in the country's largest native-title claim, covering the land from Wentworth to Wanaaring in the state's northwest, and including all of the Lower Darling country and a 400-kilometre stretch of the river. It gave them not ownership but right of access to land and water to practise their traditional laws and customs. In Barkandji tradition, nearly all of those laws and customs are about the Barka. They are the Barkandji, the people of the river.

At the same time as fighting the native-title claim, the Barkandji had been "consulted" over the Murray–Darling Basin Plan – "fake consultation," elder Badger Bates calls it, because nobody ever listened and nothing they said changed the result. When the native-title decision was released, Bates noted that the river was already unusually low, and the mental and physical health of the Barkandji was being affected. He didn't know about the changes to the water resource plan when he said that. Today, his view is that the river has, quite literally, been stolen.

*

The people of the Lower Darling were still getting across what had been done to them with the water resource plan when another aspect of the Murray–Darling Basin Plan was brought home to them.

On Google Earth, the Menindee Lakes appear like blue-green beads on the string of the river. On the schematic maps put out by the Authority – which look like a diagram of household plumbing, rather than a natural system – they are shown as four perfect circles, two coloured in blue to indicate their role as main storages in the system. Neither the satellite image nor the map does the lakes justice. They are vast depressions in the landscape, 25,000 years old, and one of the places in Australia where you can feel the ancient history of the land. They were almost totally dry when I visited, dotted with feral goats and cattle searching for feed. The trees, as the singer Tony Smith put it, were "dropping leaves like tears." When the lakes are full, they come alive with waterbirds and fish. They are a nursery for golden and silver perch. People from Broken Hill come here with boats.

Today the Menindee Lakes are part of the plumbing imposed on the landscape. They are gated with weirs and spillways. They can store about 2000 gigalitres, but they are very shallow. In a system desperate for more water, the losses from evaporation – up to about 420 gigalitres a year – cannot be tolerated. So it is that the Menindee Lakes are one of the most important schemes in what, in the dead, flat language of water managers, is called the sustainable diversion limit adjustment mechanism, or SDLAM. (I shouted those desiccated words – sustainable diversion limit adjustment mechanism – to the winds in the middle of the Menindee Lakes, but failed to impress the goats.)

In the Byzantine and bitter fights among the states that led to the Murray–Darling Basin Plan, it appeared there was an unbridgeable gap between South Australia on the one hand and New South Wales on the other. The SDLAM process was part of the fix. South Australia wanted 3200 gigalitres recovered for the environment. New South Wales and Victoria wanted the number to be closer to 2100. They settled on 2750, on the understanding that this would be reviewed. It was agreed that the states would recover an extra 450 gigalitres of water through efficiency measures, with this to be delivered to South Australia to maintain the health of the river. Later it was also agreed that the SDL – the cap on use – could be *lifted* through projects designed to save water or else to improve the environmental management of the river without more water. This is the sustainable diversion limit adjustment mechanism. The SDLAM process is a high-stakes game. If the projects don't go ahead, or don't recover the promised water, then farmers will, at least in theory, have to give up more water in 2024. The pressure to get the projects done, or at least the savings counted, is immense. The compact between the states relies on it.

The Menindee Lakes scheme is one of the most important water-saving projects. Like the whole of the SDLAM process, it is the result of political imperatives and compromises. The projects are running behind time, and many details of the plans remain unclear. Thirty-six projects from across the Basin were presented to federal parliament in 2018. They lacked detailed business plans, and the claimed water savings seemed little more than guesses. The Wentworth Group of Concerned Scientists assessed that only one project met the necessary conditions for approval, and twenty-five, representing up to 436 gigalitres of water recovery, should not be approved, including because of the risk to the environment.

At Menindee Lakes, the idea is to reconfigure the lakes and drain the main storage, Lake Menindee, more quickly and more often. This will, the NSW government says, save about 106 gigalitres of water a year. But many details still remain unclear. It could be an environmental catastrophe. When the Authority assessed the project in 2017, it said it might be a disaster for native fish. Eight thousand hectares of golden perch nursery in Lake Cawndilla would be lost for 65 per cent of the time. The scheme might save water, but it would not satisfy the test of doing so without environmental damage.

The South Australian royal commission report included a case study of the Menindee Lakes project as an example of the SDLAM process. Commissioner Walker concluded not only that it was "a dispiriting instance of environmental infrastructure project planning," but also that it might not be lawful, because there was no evidence to show that it would have "equivalent environmental outcomes" to recovering water from farmers. Walker said the efficiency projects had been applied in a way that was "the opposite of open, transparent and accountable government decision-making." He recommended that instead of relying on dubious efficiency savings, most of the water still to be clawed back for the environment should simply be bought from farmers. But by then it was too late. The Menindee Lakes project was law.

Meanwhile, when Barnaby Joyce became agriculture minister and, later, water minister in the Abbott government, there was an important policy shift towards the dubious efficiency measures as the main way of recovering water. In 2015, Joyce imposed a limit on water buybacks, and stated that these would be, from then on, "strategic." Wong's water buybacks had been done, for the most part, by open tender. Now negotiations were behind closed doors, conducted with little transparency.

South Australia grew increasingly concerned that there was no commitment to delivering its promised 450 gigalitres. In November 2016, Joyce wrote a letter to the Labor South Australian water minister, Ian Hunter, in which he backtracked on 450 gigalitres. Shortly after the letter, the Murray–Darling Ministerial Council met in Adelaide. Hunter and Joyce were part of a group that went for dinner at Rigoni's Bistro. The Royal Commission report later described the dinner: "The South Australian Minister made his and perhaps the then state government's views known to his interstate and Commonwealth colleagues in unambiguous terms, with Minister Hunter apparently telling Minister Joyce, in colloquial terms, to leave the jurisdiction." The Adelaide media was less circumspect. It reported that Hunter had told Joyce, and the Victorian water minister, Lisa Neville, to fuck off.

Meanwhile, Lower Darling locals are still trying to work out exactly what is going to be done to the Menindee Lakes. The retirement of the irrigation properties, the Broken Hill pipeline, the interception of low flows upstream, the intention to more frequently drain the lakes – all of it has convinced them that the intention is to accept the death of the Lower Darling as the price of New South Wales achieving its water savings. They tried to lobby, they tried to be heard. The towns of the Lower Darling are divided between two vast state electorates: Murray and Barwon. Both were then held by the National Party. Federally, the Lower Darling is in the vast federal electorate of Parkes, held by National Party MP Mark Coulton. All three politicians were lobbied, but nobody seemed to be listening.

People were getting desperate. Tony Smith's song became the implicit anthem of the region.

> Won't someone please take me
> Where I can be heard?

And then came the fish kill.

*

Graeme McCrabb, Menindee grape grower and fisherman, is an unlikely media strategist. Broad-accented, with a face weathered by the sun and a hat straight out of a Drysdale painting, he had never had much to do with journalists before December 2018. He knew things were bad with the river. He had been part of some of the so-called consultations. A few months before, he had been at a community meeting and had quizzed a Basin Authority official. There had been a number of releases from the

Menindee Lakes to promote fish breeding in 2016, and now the lakes had not recharged, which meant the river was drying up and there were no reserves. What priority, he asked, was being given to providing the young fish spawned with such care somewhere viable to live? The way he remembers it, the question was handballed to NSW Fisheries and not adequately answered on the night.

Then, a few weeks later, in mid-December, he went down to the river in the morning to tend his pump. There he found two Murray Cod – the iconic big fish of the river – floating dead, together with some perch. He rang and reported it to Fisheries. A few days later, on 15 December, he went back down and found the upturned bellies of perch. He was devastated. His voice still cracks when he recounts it. "It was just so sad … you can't put it into words. It was really tough, to be honest. I was sitting there, and I guess there was a bit of guilt there. Like a generational thing. Like, 'Look what we've done to the river in just 150 years.' And I've got kids. To be the generation that left the river in a worse state than what we found it, that's pretty daunting."

McCrabb and other locals decided the world needed to know what was happening. He took photos and videos with his mobile phone. He remembers a sense of desperation. "There I was standing by the river trying to ring these newsrooms, with shit telephone reception, and I was trying to tell them what was happening. And at first they were like, 'Dead fish? Yeah, okay.'" The breakthrough came when he got through to ABC Broken Hill and a young journalist, Sara Tomevska, who was having a baptism of fire since arriving a few months previously. It was her first experience of rural Australia. Tomevska wrote a story for the local radio news as well as some copy for Sydney. She was on her way home that afternoon when she got a call from the national newsroom. The Menindee locals were putting startling pictures on social media. Would she go out to the site of the fish kill the next day?

The people of the Lower Darling had devised a strategy that would do professional lobbyists proud. They agreed some lines. This was not only the drought, they would say. This was due to the mismanagement of the $13-billion Murray–Darling Basin Plan. "Thirteen billion to get dead fish ... We agreed those lines and we stuck to them," recalls McCrabb.

The ABC story made the national news, as well as dominating local bulletins. Tomevska went back to Sydney for her Christmas holidays. The night before she returned to Broken Hill, in early January, there was a second fish kill. She went straight from the plane the following morning to a long, hot drive to Menindee, then into a boat with McCrabb. It was 45 degrees Celsius, and they were plying a silver path between the corpses of fish. Tomevska recalls: "It was just as far as you could see big grey Murray Cod floating to the surface. It was apocalyptic, almost. It didn't feel real. It was surreal." Where the fish piled up against the bank, the flies were already at work. "The smell was incredible."

McCrabb found himself being interviewed by some of the country's leading journalists. He appeared in a video standing bare-chested, waist-high in water, cradling a giant dead Murray cod as though it were his child. "I probably didn't appreciate it at the time, the seniority of the journalists I was talking to," he says. But he put all their mobile numbers in his phone. He had a feeling they would come in handy. He was learning a new respect for journalists, and their impact on the workings of politics. He watched Tomevska working fourteen-hour days in the heat, surrounded by the smell of dead fish. In a quiet moment by the side of the river, in the middle of the stink, he asked if she was okay. She said she was, and they fell into silent reflection at the enormity of it all.

Politicians were beginning to come to Menindee. The NSW minister for water, Niall Blair, turned up on 15 January. About 150 locals waving placards were hoping to grill him, but the closest they got was when he sped past in a boat, stirring up the corpses of fish in his wake. He said he had received threats on social media and was advised by police to stay out of reach of the locals. The police denied they had given any such advice. He fronted the cameras downstream, and blamed the drought for the fish deaths. It had nothing to do with extractions upstream.

The third fish kill, on 28 January, was the worst. McCrabb knew it was coming. "I started the day with two coffees because I knew it was on." It had turned cold overnight, and the immediate cause of the deaths was a cooling of the temperature, leading to mixing up of the water in the river, and oxygen depletion. He went down to the river, and it was silver with dead fish. By now he had all the contact numbers. He rang Tomevska and journalists throughout the nation. She came out from Broken Hill again, and other journalists began to arrive. Most of the images that Australians remember come from this fish kill. Tomevska remembers that over thirty kilometres, "from one side of the river to the other, dead fish, it was completely white, as though everything that was in the river had risen to the surface."

Some fish were buried in pits. Tomevska climbed into the pit, avoiding splashback from the corpses, to film segments for the 7 p.m. news bulletin. Now the international media were getting interested. The locals, in the stench on the banks of the dying river, were sending their pictures and videos to the world. Tomevska remembers interviewing "deeply engaged and visibly upset" NSW Fisheries staff, but the politicians were more reluctant. "They were concerned, and they acknowledged the level of the environmental catastrophe. But they didn't want to engage with the idea that it was the Plan, or water policy in New South Wales. They wanted to say it was the drought and only the drought."

Then the South Australian royal commission report was released. On that day, the NSW deputy premier and leader of the Nationals, John Barilaro, was in Menindee. At a community meeting, he attacked Tomevska for asking why the premier, Gladys Berejiklian, had not come. He said the purpose of the meeting was for him to talk to the community, not journalists. "I just said I thought the community would like answers to the question too," says Tomevska, "and they all said, 'Yes, right on.'" At her back were the local irrigators, the Barkandji community, the townsfolk, and it was an angry room. Afterwards, Barilaro gave a media conference on the banks of the river. He said he hadn't read the South Australian report but it was "self-interested." And by now, Barilaro was issuing some of the first of many threats that New South Wales would quit the Murray–Darling Basin Plan.

The Australian Academy of Science was asked by the then Leader of the Opposition, Bill Shorten, to investigate the causes of the fish kill. Its report concluded the immediate cause was deoxygenation of the water. But the underlying cause was that there was simply not enough water in the river – the result of several factors, including drought and excessive diversions upstream. The fact that the Menindee Lakes had been drained, part of the attempt to minimise evaporation losses, meant there were no reserves of water to save the fish. The Academy of Science report expressed strong support for the *Water Act* and the Basin Plan, with their intentions to increase water for the environment, but concluded there were "serious deficiencies in governance and management, which collectively have eroded the intent."

The fish kill became an issue in the NSW state election. In the lead-up to the March 2019 poll, the towns of the Lower Darling were suddenly a target of spending. For example, there was a commitment of $25 million in federal and state funding to seal the road between Pooncarie and Menindee, which the community had been wanting for years to encourage tourism. On election day, the National Party lost the two seats covering the Lower Darling – Barwon and Murray – to the Shooters, Fishers and Farmers Party. The Menindee locals don't claim complete credit for this. Their numbers are too low to have directly swung the result, but their success in publicising the fish kill had bolstered the impression across rural New South Wales that the National Party had abandoned farmers and country people in the south of the state, because it was too beholden to its upstream, cotton-growing networks.

Roy Butler, who won Barwon on a 19.5 per cent swing against the Nationals, is well liked on the Lower Darling. The electorate is vast, covering more than 40 per cent of New South Wales – from Broken Hill to the Queensland border and east to Narrabri. Nevertheless, he shows up on the Lower Darling often. Before the election he seemed to be at every community meeting. He is across the politics of the river at an intimate level – and there is a good reason for this. His adviser, John Clements, is a former member of the Murray–Darling Basin Authority's Northern Basin Advisory Committee, a former head of industry group Namoi Water and a former adviser to independent federal MP Tony Windsor.

Helen Dalton, the Shooters and Fishers member for Murray, has her electorate offices far away in Deniliquin and Griffith. She has rarely been seen on the Lower Darling and is not well liked. The story of her election concerns the other branch of the tree of the Murray–Darling, and different kinds of capacity to be heard.

The election of Dalton and Butler signalled a new kind of politics around water.

*

So did those few weeks of being heard, of making world headlines, change things on the Lower Darling?

One of the benefits, if that is the right word, of being so comprehensively screwed is the alliances that have formed between the Barkandji and the irrigators. I wondered if some of the Barkandji were censoring themselves, suppressing hostility to the invader. There was no sign of such hostility. Cindy Bates told Graeme McCrabb in my hearing, "You're mob." From the Barkandji, I heard the complaints about the end of low flows for irrigators and what the end of those businesses would mean for the seasonal jobs that used to be done by Aboriginal people. From the irrigators, I heard concerns about the waterholes, and the home of the Rainbow Serpent. Funding has flowed to this region for the road, for a tourism centre – for everything but a change in the allocation of water.

When I visited in mid-December 2019, Fisheries staff were using electricity to stun fish in the few remaining pools on the Darling, and then gathering them up and transporting them downstream to Wentworth in a desperate attempt to save them. Diesel-fuelled pumps were sitting on the riverbank throwing water into the air in an attempt to maintain oxygen levels.

Everyone expected more fish to die over the summer. Graeme McCrabb was ready. Watching the aerators – noisy things – he reflected that if aliens visited earth, they'd find it pretty bizarre. An environmental tragedy caused partly by climate change, "and we are burning fossil fuels to oxygenate water and truck fish around. I reckon they'd say you don't deserve to have this place. I reckon they'd say we're taking it over and serves you bloody right."

So what's happening with the Menindee Lakes project?

The chief executive of the Basin Authority, Phillip Glyde, has been to Pooncarie and Menindee. Not surprisingly, he found "deep suspicion, and absolutely no trust whatsoever in any government entity." He admits to frustration. The detail of the Menindee Lakes plan remains unclear, and the NSW government, he says, "hasn't really started the consultation process in any serious way." The SDLAM efficiency projects as a whole are moving very slowly. "We're very worried that while some projects have progressed, the major ones that make the difference aren't progressing quickly enough to meet the 2024 deadline."

The Commonwealth Environmental Water Holder, Jody Swirepik, can see the appeal of the Menindee Lakes project. The loss from evaporation is high. But, she says, there is more at stake than water savings. Other benefits and impacts should also be considered. "The evaporation savings depend on keeping water out of some lakes and the water being released more quickly and more often. But the local people want water to be kept in the lakes. Would the changes to the lakes mean the Darling ceases to flow more often? And how do you balance all that? The project needs to weigh up all of these issues. This is what New South Wales needs to work out," she says. Is she frustrated at how long this is taking? She agrees that New South Wales has been slow to have the "critical discussion" about broadening the objectives of the project.

New South Wales has to complete this project or extract more savings from farmers. That is the imperative driving what, on the scanty information publicly available, looks like an environmental catastrophe. From my discussions with the water bureaucrats, it is clear that negotiations are going on behind the scenes. But in the meantime, as one local said to me: "It's like that line from *Apocalypse Now*. They are destroying the river in order to save it."

Meanwhile, I had met people who believed the Darling River had not disappeared, but was being kept from them, upstream.

I went looking for it.

The 320 kilometres of road from Wilcannia to Bourke, hugging the Darling River, is grey bulldust between saltbush plains. The stock has been removed because of the drought. Feral goats and kangaroos are the only things moving, and cattlegrids the only reminder the country is claimed, and owned. About thirty kilometres out of Wilcannia there is a cross by the side of the road, surrounded by plastic flowers. Children's handprints decorate an old board. There is a story here, obviously, of loss and grief, impenetrable to those not directly involved. Someone has planted a tree and draped it with Christmas decorations, but the tree is dead.

This is the kind of road where one lifts a finger from the steering wheel to acknowledge the drivers of the very few approaching vehicles – mostly trucks. Why do Australians do this, on our remote roads? I like to think it is an implicit acknowledgement that we are in it together: that if I was in trouble, you would help, and I would help you. After what I had seen and heard around the Menindee Lakes, this reflection led to a small lift in my spirits.

I drove through Tilpa: population nine. A memorial to the locals who served in the Boer War, including former local Breaker Morant, is the main point of interest. The town's name is a signifier of the country. "Tilpa" comes from the Barkandji word *thulpa*, meaning floodwaters. In a wet year, the river can spread out up to seventy kilometres. The people who farm here are floodplain pastoralists, growing lamb, beef, fodder and, increasingly, goats for meat on the pasture that reaches for the skies when the floodwater recedes. Justin and Julie McClure of Kallara Station took a photo of the flood in March 2012. It shows sheets of water in all directions. They had been isolated for weeks. A trip to Tilpa took forty minutes by boat, rather than the usual fifteen-minute drive. But now the station is dry, their small garden the only green.

Onward to Louth. The population is only forty-five, but there is a 130-kilometre bitumen connection to the outside world, running south to Cobar. That means the pub, a rambling building on the riverbank, does a good trade from tourists. There is also a decent dirt road onwards to Bourke. But I took the bad dirt road, on the other side of the river, because at Kallara Station when I told Julie McClure that I was looking for the Darling, she suggested I go to Toorale.

In September 2008 – less than a year after the election that brought Kevin Rudd to power and made Penny Wong water minister – it was announced that the Commonwealth and New South Wales would buy the vast Toorale Station at a cost of $24 million. The station itself was to become a national park. It was one of the first and most controversial water buybacks in the "Pennies from Heaven" period.

Toorale was not just any station. In its time it was a miracle – evidence of dominion over nature, of success in taming the great brown land. At the junction of the Warrego and Darling rivers, drawing its water from branches reaching up past Charleville, Toorale could have been the template for every outback station that has made its way into Australian literature – for Drogheda in *The Thorn Birds*, for example. Henry Lawson worked here as a roustabout in 1892. Toorale was also a centre for the battles between shearers and pastoralists, part of the history of the rise of unionism and the birth of the Australian Labor Party. Toorale is a remnant of the dream and reality of gardens in the desert. Its founder, Samuel McCaughey, sank some of the earliest artesian bores and built huge levy banks and dams. He captured the flow of the Warrego and remoulded the landscape, creating great wetlands and irrigating pasture that allowed Toorale, at its height, to be the largest sheep station in the world.

The old station building is now a museum – deserted when I visited. It sits by the river, a rambling verandaed haven surrounded by outbuildings, the remnants of its life as a centre for "civilisation" in the country literally back of Bourke. Nearby was the camp of the Kurnu-Barkandji people, who worked on the station, still living on country.

When Wong bought the water, local farmers claimed turning Toorale into a national park would devastate the Bourke region. It was anti-rural, they said, and a "sop to the Green movement." Toorale was a big local employer, but also a symbol – more than just a business. Across the Basin, buying water for the river was enormously controversial. Rural communities blamed the buybacks for causing what they said was a Swiss cheese effect – leaving others to bear the cost of the infrastructure, while also creating holes in communities that depended on irrigation revenue and jobs. Wong was blamed for hastening the collapse of towns, ending whole industries. She was burned in effigy at demonstrations in Griffith.

There are six major dams on Toorale. They have altered the flow of the Warrego for over 100 years. Wong announced that, as a result of the purchase, 20 gigalitres of water would be returned to the Darling, and up to 80 gigalitres in a flood year. It would turn around the long-term decline of the once great river, she said. Justin McClure, the floodplain harvester who lives downstream, knows Toorale perhaps better than anyone. He thinks the Wong purchase has helped the river. There is water seen in the Darling that was not there before. But the full benefits have yet to appear.

I turned a corner on the road through Toorale, and suddenly there was water everywhere, flowing across the road, making me unsure whether I could drive on. My travelling companion waded in it to gauge the depth. Water came up to his knees. We drove across, hearts in our mouths, and felt the flow tug at our vehicle.

How to describe the impact of seeing this water, after so many hundred kilometres of dry riverbeds and despair? It was shocking, almost distressing. I didn't know whether to celebrate or get angry. Had I found the Darling? Is this where it was being kept? What was this water doing here? Where did it come from? Where was it going?

Weeks later, in Canberra, I told the Commonwealth Environmental Water Holder, Jody Swirepik, that the water I saw on Toorale was the most I had seen anywhere in one place in the Northern Basin. Where had it come from, and why was it there rather than downstream in the parched communities?

The answer is complicated. When the water licences for Toorale were purchased, it was agreed that the dams were to be "reviewed" for modification or demolition. There was no commitment to demolish them all. The Commonwealth owned the water, or some of it – but managing the land and the dams was the job of the state government. Some of the local farmers hold rights to the water being stored in some of the dams. They oppose their demolition. Meanwhile, the NSW government's assessment of "heritage values," including of the artificial wetland habitat created by the main Boera Dam, has also stood in the way.

When I visited Toorale, the Warrego was one of the few rivers running in the Northern Basin, thanks to rainfall further north from Cyclone Trevor. The water I saw crossing the road – part of about 30 gigalitres that made it to Toorale – was the last of it. In the weeks before I arrived, the biggest dam – Peebles – had finally been "decommissioned," meaning the wall had been knocked down. But the other dams remain standing. Some of them, said Swirepik, are "important in a cultural heritage sense." The Commonwealth and NSW governments can't and shouldn't just "punch through" cultural heritage issues, she said.

But what about other cultural heritage issues? What about the Barkandji's native title rights, the Rainbow Serpent, and the state of the Menindee Lakes? What about the lack of drinking water in Wilcannia? Swirepik said it is likely only a small amount of water, about 3 gigalitres, would have reached the Menindee Lakes if there had been no dams. This would not have been enough to flow into the Lower Darling.

There are triggers that determine the balance between using the water locally and meeting needs downstream. When it is very dry, the priority is to release as much water as possible to the Darling for "critical human needs." The hard reality is, as Swirepik acknowledges, that the old pipes through the Toorale dams connecting them to the river are too small. The water passes through at just 600 megalitres a day, which removes the peak of the flow. As a result it doesn't travel very far. By the time it hits the Darling, it is a trickle.

It is up to New South Wales to demolish the dams or put in bigger pipes, or both. Is Swirepik frustrated at the time it is taking? She is tactful: "I am conscious that the government has not been able to deliver the outcomes that people sought in a timely enough way."

It's a tragedy, or an irony, or both. Here on Toorale, in the country most Australians would call the middle of nowhere, the legacy of Samuel McCaughey and his victory over the land stands in the way of the ambitions of our own time – to undo our mistakes, to make our future sustainable, and to save the river.

*

Toorale is not the only challenge facing the management of environmental water. The maps put out by the Murray–Darling Basin Authority show a firm delineation between the Northern and Southern Basins. The line runs more or less west from near Bathurst at the foot of the Great Dividing Range, then follows the Lower Darling from Wilcannia to Louth. The people of the Lower Darling are thus in an in-between land – sometimes north and sometimes south, depending on the bank of the river.

The divide between the Southern and Northern Basins is not only about geography. It is also a sociological divide, a political divide and a divide in regulation. The Southern Basin, in the rather contemptuous words of one northern cotton grower, is a place of "tidy rivers. I think of them as kind of being behind a white picket fence, all very nice and clean and predictable." In the south – say, around Griffith and Leeton – any traveller can see the small forests of meters – high-tech, with alarm systems to prevent tampering, their solar panels facing to the sky. In the north, on the other hand, the Authority estimates that up to 75 per cent of the water diverted is unmetered. Most of the allegations of water theft and dubious water purchase deals by the Commonwealth concern the Northern Basin.

The north has also been one of the main challenges to the management of the water owned by the taxpayer and intended for the environment. The volume of water taken by irrigators is calculated, often, with an honesty system of logbooks. The right to pump is triggered by the level of the river. Sometimes there are meters as well, but many are old-fashioned and not regularly checked. The problem is that if environmental water is released upstream, it raises the height of the river downstream and triggers the right to pump. The Commonwealth might buy water, or release water from a dam, but it is powerless to protect it once it enters the next management area.

Bill Johnson is a former employee of the Murray–Darling Basin Authority turned critic. He used to be an environmental water manager and is now a Dubbo-based consultant. He claims: "We were lying to people. We bought water in some of the rivers, the Macquarie, the Namoi and the Gwydir, but because of the different Plan areas, the water comes down the Namoi and goes into the Barwon–Darling and is no longer protected." He says he has notes of a meeting on the Namoi at which irrigators questioned why the government was buying 10 per cent of their water when they knew it was just going to be pumped out by other irrigators downstream. I heard similar stories from five farmers in the Northern Basin: water bought from them, or clawed back through efficiency schemes, being released for an environmental flow, only to disappear when it crossed the border to the next management area. Johnson says when he asked, "Why we are lying to people?" he was told that thanks to the cap on diversions – the sustainable diversion limit – it would work out in the long term and on average. That, he says, is "just bullshit. It's really hard to make sense of it. It's Alice in Wonderland stuff, in the sense that it's really disorienting. You know how Alice had to run really fast just to stay in the same place? It's like that. How do we know that it will work out in the long term, on averages? They say it's because the models tell us so. But in the Northern Basin, the models are simply not fit for purpose. We don't know enough." And, he says, averages are near meaningless to the real-world management of a river in a system that is so variable.

Swirepik acknowledges the issue, but she also claims that environmental flows have been accessed by irrigators on "only a handful" of occasions.

And, she says, the Water Holder has got better at working with the states to "shepherd" water through the system. The best example of this, and the one that she likes to talk about, is the "Northern Connectivity Event" of April 2018. Thirty gigalitres of water stored from the wet spring of 2016 was released from the Copeton Dam on the Gwydir River and the Glenlyon Dam near the Queensland–NSW border. The aim was to get the flow down to Wilcannia, linking up the river system to protect and support native fish, refreshing the waterholes over 2000 kilometres. At the beginning of 2018, people had been playing cricket in the bed of the Darling River at Tilpa. By June, the cricket pitch was underwater. Later that month, 7.5 gigalitres of the water reached Wilcannia, having travelled 1700 kilometres. The Wilcannia community had a party, including a traditional dance by the river, as it went past. As it worked its way through the system, water was absorbed into the dry riverbeds, re-wetting the banks, boosting water quality and giving native plants a drink. About 2 gigalitres made it into the Menindee Lakes. The water had been carefully tracked, including by using satellite imagery. Any "losses" as the water travelled were due to seepage and evaporation, and not because of any unauthorised pumping.

The NSW government protected the flow with a temporary embargo on pumping. It was quite an achievement, and Swirepik counts it as a success – and a learning opportunity. But the whole enterprise relied on the goodwill of the NSW government. The Murray–Darling Basin Plan was "macro reform," and what is now needed, says Swirepik, is "micro reform" to make sure that environmental water flows are protected. That would take agreement from the states. Swirepik says a lot of work has been done on this. But at the moment New South Wales is threatening to pull out of the Murray–Darling Basin Plan. How confident is Swirepik that New South Wales will continue to play nice with environmental water?

Swirepik is very careful with her words. It was clear to me that while the political rhetoric is white hot, on the ground and behind the scenes the bureaucrats have been cooperating. But if New South Wales leaves the plan, it seems there is no guarantee that will continue. Swirepik cautiously acknowledges that in the future protecting environmental water bought at taxpayer expense might be "challenging."

Rain had fallen near Bourke. You might remember the Facebook video that went viral – a farmer stripped down to his undies, hollering and dancing in the puddles. The rain was not enough to break the drought, but it transformed the landscape for a week or so. The colours turned vivid. It was as though a paintbrush of green had been splattered over red canvas.

Upstream of Bourke, on the Barwon River at Brewarrina, I stopped at what are claimed to be the oldest human-made structures in the world and probably some of the first examples of aquaculture. The rock fish-traps are twelve teardrop-shaped pools at different levels across half a kilometre of riverbed. The Ngemba people would herd fish through the small openings, then block them. Around 1970, a weir was built virtually over the top of the fish traps, to provide a water supply for the town. The pouring of the concrete destroyed some of the traps, and today the weir looms over the rest. People say that European carp have overrun the river downstream. When I visited, the traps were dry and bottled water was being trucked into Brewarrina. There was a small pond of water behind the weir, so salty it was hard to drink.

This is the upstream system. Here are the irrigators who are the beneficiaries of those late, controversial changes to the Barwon–Darling Water Resource Plan. Here, too, are some of the irrigators who were charged with water theft after the *Four Corners* program – such as one of the state's biggest cotton growers, Peter Harris, who is awaiting verdicts in two cases against him, and Anthony Barlow, who pleaded guilty to pumping during an embargo, but claimed he had been told by the water minister at the time, Kevin Humphries, that pumping was permitted.

Here, too, is Brewarrina mayor Phillip O'Connor, a larger-than-life man – big belly, big beard, big personality – known locally as Ocker. He claims to fear for his life because he was one of the key sources for *Four Corners*.

O'Connor took the ABC reporters in his boat and pointed out the giant pumps. He showed them diary entries and videos of times he had seen his neighbours' pumps running when pumping was not allowed. Later, O'Connor wrote a submission on behalf of Brewarrina Shire Council to the South Australian royal commission. He said the net result of the Murray–Darling Basin Plan had been decreased water security for communities. Water licences that had once been "sleepers" had been revived so they could be sold, and environmental flows were routinely diverted and mismanaged. He claimed to know of one case in which water had been pumped illegally because the river was too low but records of river heights had been retrospectively adjusted after allegations were made. Most water users were honest, he said, but the systems were flawed. "Self-interested parties clearly have access to the policy makers."

This, too, is part of the political boundary between north and south – a network of political influence, the product of history, markets and crops.

The *Four Corners* program "Pumped" screened on 24 July 2017. In the cities, it passed quickly from memory. In the Murray–Darling Basin, it is talked about as though it happened only weeks ago. The ramifications are still playing out. The program carried an audio recording of a teleconference between the top water bureaucrat in New South Wales, Gavin Hanlon, and irrigator groups, in which an official offered special access to restricted government information, advantaging them in their negotiations with government. The program alleged that Hanlon had prevented an operation on non-compliant irrigators urged upon him by his own investigators.

The corruption allegations were referred to the NSW Independent Commission Against Corruption. Nobody knows when the ICAC will report. One irrigator met me in Bourke and, mixing his metaphors, declared this "a sleeping bombshell." The NSW Ombudsman issued a special report in response to the ABC program. As well, the NSW government appointed retired senior public servant Ken Matthews to conduct an independent inquiry. Both reports were damning. Water compliance had been ineffectual and needed significant improvement. Allegations of water theft had not been acted on – sometimes for years. Metering of water take was poor, and there was evidence of meter-tampering. Environmental water was not being protected. Transparency was lacking.

The NSW government acted quickly on Matthews' interim report, accepting in principle all his recommendations. There was to be a new policy – no meter, no pump, and increased transparency about water usage. But by the time of Matthews' final report, he was already concerned about "increasing pressure from certain stakeholders to water down" the changes. Action was "insufficiently urgent and lacks detail."

After submissions from the NSW Irrigators' Council, the NSW government introduced exceptions to the "no meter no pump" rule and details of key transparency measures – including a public register of water licences – were postponed. Originally, the deadline for the "no meter no pump" rule was December 2019. Meters would have to meet the latest standards and have the ability to transmit real-time data to the authorities. That deadline has now been extended to December 2020 for most users. Irrigator groups argued that it was going to take too long to supply and install the meters, and that, given the drought, it was impossible to calibrate them due to a lack of water.

The *Four Corners* program wasn't the end of the ABC's role in Northern Basin politics. Later in 2017, *Lateline* screened a program detailing allegations by Goondiwindi farmer Chris Lamey concerning his neighbour, cotton farmer John Norman – who happened to be the second cousin of the wife of the federal minister for water, David Littleproud. Lamey's farm, Coomonga, is on the Macintyre River on the Queensland border. He is a floodplain farmer. Every eighteen months or so, the river would flood, water would lie on his property for a few days and then he could plant. In 2015, that began to change. In the floods that year, water stayed on his property much longer. When he investigated, he found that Norman Farming had built a bridge on the river, with earthworks each side that were constricting the flow. Lamey consulted the NSW authorities and was told that the bridge didn't need development approval. In 2016, there was another flood and it took three weeks for the water to leave Lamey's property. The back-up, Lamey discovered, was caused by about 50 kilometres of levies and earthworks on the Norman farm. Lamey spent months trying to get action. He made numerous complaints to council, which retrospectively approved some of the earthworks. He took a Supreme Court legal action and made approaches to state and federal politicians, but little was done until the *Lateline* program.

Meanwhile, a criminal investigation was underway. Between 2010 and 2017, Norman had received up to $31 million under a scheme called "Healthy Headwaters." This was one of the water efficiency grant schemes that had been part of the deal cut by Wong and Rudd in 2008 to get the states to agree to refer their powers to the Commonwealth. The money had been doled out by the Queensland government, with virtually no scrutiny of the projects. John Norman and his chief financial officer are currently facing charges of defrauding the Commonwealth for allegedly using the money granted from Healthy Headwaters – meant to fund the installation of efficient irrigation systems – to complete earthworks on his property.

*

What Norman was doing, with his levies, was an example of floodplain harvesting: the capturing of water that flows across land in a flood. Floodplain harvesting is one of the great unknowns of the Murray–Darling Basin. It has been either partly regulated or unregulated – never fully measured or accounted for. Nobody knows how much of the rainfall is intercepted and, largely out of sight of the public and of regulators, put into storage behind levy banks and in so-called ring tank dams – big, earthen embankment storages built on flat land.

When the Basin Plan was written, it was estimated that floodplain diversions accounted for about 210 gigalitres of water use. In Senate Estimates in October 2019, the Authority's Dr Peta-Joanne Derham said that was certainly an underestimate. "In fact, in some New South Wales catchments it's above what we would believe would be legal take." When floodplain harvesting is fully accounted for, the Authority says, the sustainable diversion limits will have to increase to take account of it. But for now, the water is counted as "losses" in its modelling. This raises many questions. If so much water can be counted as "losses," what does that say for the quality of the models that calculate seepage, evaporation and transpiration? If the water has not been "lost" but lies in the giant earthen-walled tanks on the black soil plains of northern New South Wales, it is not flowing downstream, or connecting floodplain to river, or river to downstream. It is not recharging aquifers. It is a national resource, held for private benefit, at unknown levels, "above legal take."

Nobody knows how much is involved, but some of the guesses have been frightening. Australian Floodplain Association president Terry Korn was quoted in *The Land* in March 2019 claiming it could be as much as 3000 gigalitres. If he is right, it is a staggering figure – more than the total amount so far recovered for the environment under the Plan. The irrigation industry has ridiculed the 3000 gigalitre suggestion, while others have suggested it might be even higher.

Now the push is on to measure and regulate floodplain harvesting. It's a complicated thing to do. You can measure how much water is in storage or dams, but how do you determine where the water came from? Storages might contain river water, recycled water from the property, and water from floodplain harvesting. The aim will be, the Authority says, to restrict floodplain harvesting to the levels that were being taken in 2000. How that will be determined isn't clear. Some fear that licensing floodplain harvesting and then trying to peg it back will result in people being compensated for ceasing to do something they shouldn't have done in the first place.

Drink in the pubs of the border rivers region of New South Wales and Queensland and ask about water theft, floodplain harvesting and John Norman, and on the first beer you will be told everyone is compliant. Or at least, they will tell you, people in *this* area, on this river, are compliant. Don't know about those jokers over there, on another river, or downstream or upstream. On the third beer, you hear the stories: a container dumped in a local creek to bank up the water. A billabong that was full a week ago and suddenly empty – where has the water gone? Those with properties close to town complain that while their pumps, logbooks and meters are regularly checked, those further out operate with less scrutiny. "Everyone cheats a little bit," I was told. "Some more than others." And what is cheating anyway? One irrigator said to me: "I have a little ephemeral creek running across my property, and it joins the river just where I have my pump. So am I pumping out of that creek, which is unregulated, and doing floodplain harvesting, or am I pumping from the river?" It was pointed out to me that while one needs a permit to build a dam or a levee bank with which to store water, you can build a road on your farm without needing any approval. Naturally, you don't want that road to flood – so you build it high, on an earth bank. And there you are – de facto water storage when the floods come, and no permit required. How will that be regulated?

Metering is inconsistent, but even old pumps have seals to prevent tampering. However, I was told, "every maintenance man has a box of spare seals in the back of his ute." A seal can be broken, the meter "adjusted" and another seal put in its place. Or, where the system runs on logbooks – the length of time a pump runs, with the volume taken judged by the size of the pipe and the pump – one might run that pump a bit harder than its theoretical capacity, getting more water in the hour than the records will reflect.

There is a lot of talk about the new high-tech meters that are coming in the aftermath of the *Four Corners* program and the Matthews inquiry. It is rumoured that although you "talk to these new meters with a computer, not a screwdriver," you could for the price of a slab of beer get the installer to let you know the access code. The instructions for how to use that code to access the data were all on the manufacturer's website. If you were smart with a computer, it was suggested, perhaps they were not tamper-proof after all. Somebody – "not me, of course" – was bound to try.

When the Plan was devised, there were serious gaps in knowledge of the Northern Basin. A later review was meant to address that. But, when it was completed, it looked not only at the science and hydrology, but also at the social and economic impact of clawing back water. Far from further pegging back water use, it recommended lifting the cap on water diversions by 70 gigalitres. In return, the Queensland and NSW governments were to agree to "toolkit measures" – better management of environmental flows and construction of fishways. The South Australian royal commission was scathing about this "triple bottom line" approach – which was arguably unlawful. The science suggested that water use should be further reduced, not lifted, the commission's report said. Yet the resulting changes to the Plan were voted through in 2018, with Labor's support, in the same package that included the sustainable diversion adjustment mechanisms and the Menindee Lakes project.

*

One of the tides of hatred currently sweeping Basin communities is about crop choice.

There have always been changes to crops. Generations of South Australian teenagers – including me – earned their pocket money standing on concrete floors in corrugated-iron sheds cutting apricots in half and laying them on trays to be dried in the sun. By the time I entered university in the late 1970s, grapes were replacing much of the stone fruit. The growth of the European Economic Community had killed much of the market.

Generally, the reliable water of the Southern Basin favours permanent crops – fruits and nuts and grapes. They must be watered or they die. But in the north, the natural variability of the rivers instead leads to annual crops, and particularly, once irrigation got underway, cotton. Rice – mostly grown along the Murray and Murrumbidgee – was once the scapegoat for the Basin's problems, because it was so thirsty – grown in flooded paddocks. Then the rice farmers got smarter, using less water and growing a second crop on the saturated paddocks. In recent years, genetic engineering has meant that cotton can be grown in cooler climates, and as a result cotton has begun to replace rice in the irrigation properties of the Southern Basin.

Australian cotton farmers are good at what they do. They get 227 kilograms of cotton for every megalitre of water, compared to 138 in California, 136 in Egypt and 59 in Pakistan. Cotton has an image as a thirsty crop, but it requires less water per hectare than citrus fruit and certainly less than almond trees. Both cotton and almonds are very profitable. If decisions were made on profit alone, the Basin might soon be dominated by these two crops, wiping out more of the rice industry and most of dairying.

Centre Alliance senator for South Australia Rex Patrick has become increasingly active in water politics. The cotton farmers of Queensland almost choke at the mention of his name, because after a tour of the Northern Basin and accepting their hospitality, he put forward a bill outlawing the export of cotton. "A ridiculous publicity stunt," Dirranbandi farmer and irrigation representative Frank Deshon spat out when I asked him about it. Patrick argued that Australia was effectively exporting water, because almost all the cotton grown goes overseas. But what about almonds, which are also mainly exported – and grown in his electorate of South Australia? When I challenged him on this, he dodged the question, before saying he hadn't really meant to ban cotton, but rather to provoke a debate on agricultural policy and what crop mix should be grown, and whether the government should intervene to protect diversity.

There are two extremes to this debate – those with strong faith in free markets on the one hand, and on the other those who would like to see a managed system of agriculture, like that in the European Union, where governments intervene to protect small farms, the diversity of the landscape and the cohesion of communities.

Professor Mike Young, one of the architects of the water trading system, tends to the first view. Australian farming is run hard, he says, like a Formula One racing car, not a Model T Ford. The consequences are that it tends to run at the edge of capacity, not conservatively – but it generates enormous wealth. "If you want to see Australia's worst poverty, you head to the cities, not the bush." If governments got involved in trying to choose crops, they would be very bad at it, he argues. He sees the move from rice to cotton in the Southern Basin as an example. It has been "awful" for rice mills and those who work in them, but great for the farmers who made the switch in response to market forces. If government had been involved, it would have come under pressure to protect rice. "But the result of the change has been that the communities of the Southern Basin are much wealthier, and the country makes more money."

On the other hand, Maryanne Slattery of the Australia Institute has little time for arguments based on faith in free markets. She has argued for government to act to protect family farms, in particular dairy farms. "Our nation's food bowl has become dominated by big, often foreign-owned, business producing cotton and nuts. Is that what Australians want the food bowl of our nation to become?" She believes that, in the current drought, "emergency relief" should be provided to the Southern Basin dairy industry, now on its knees.

The ideologies that underlie this debate are complicated by the geography – the fact that the market can never be perfect. The river is not a canal. The theories play out in a landscape, which includes a political landscape. How did the Northern Basin farmers become so influential? Why is the cotton industry such an effective lobbyist? Like crop choice itself, the answer is a mix of soil, markets, history, wealth and, perhaps most of all, access to water.

Ed Fessey is a floodplain grazier north of Brewarrina on the Lower Balonne Floodplain – a system of braided streams and channels that includes the Narran Lakes, one of the indicator sites by which the Murray–Darling Basin Plan's success in improving the environment is measured. His father received the property in a ballot aimed at allocating land to returned servicemen after World War II. He lived under a coolibah tree in a tent until he could build a shanty, and later struggled and sacrificed to send his three sons away to Sydney to be educated at St Ignatius' College, Riverview. That was one of the preferred choices of wealthy farmers of rural northern New South Wales and Queensland. At Riverview, Fessey was a few years ahead of future Nationals leader Barnaby Joyce. Fessey remembers Joyce as "a problem child." Joyce's family lived on a station at Danglemah, about 60 kilometres from Tamworth, and his first job was as an accountant in the developing Queensland cotton town of St George, which was booming after the building of the Beardmore Dam. Fessey says:

> They were very conservative areas and Barnaby wasn't aware of very many other issues, or how things worked elsewhere … He could see all the developing country around St George and he thought that was the way to go. So he got into bed with all these guys and had his business going well, and he got on the gravy train and thought this was the way for the rest of the world. But the resource was quite limited and highly variable and wasn't going to deliver the outcome he thought, and he has a lot of trouble understanding that.

Fessey was on the Authority's Northern Basin Advisory Committee. He wasn't impressed by what he saw: figures being "massaged" when there was a gap between the models and actual water flows. He still believes the Plan is a worthwhile framework, but of Joyce he says, "If you see what he's done with the Basin Plan, it's like you had a drunk driver and his mates jump inside the Basin Plan and they have a great time and they roll the vehicle, and the Basin Plan is bleeding and oozing inconsistencies." Fessey thinks that to sort out the mess we need a federal royal commission. "You've got to put the judiciary through them."

Other irrigators describe the Northern Basin as being all about "the old school tie." Says Alan Whyte, the farmer from the Lower Darling, "They are wealthy people because they are very good at growing cotton, and that is a very dominant crop. Nothing wrong with that, but nobody sends their kids to the Moree high school if they can help it. They go to Kings and

Riverview and Toowoomba Grammar. You'll find the growers and the politicians all played for the same rugby team. And they stick together." Rachel Strachan, also from the Lower Darling, says that when she attended a meeting of the NSW Irrigators Council, "Lower Darling thoughts were never received well." The cotton growers were "very dominant men, and they have a dominant style, and it's sit down, this is how it's going to be."

A number of National Party politicians have backgrounds rooted in the Northern Basin and the great cotton boom. David Littleproud was born and raised in Chinchilla, on the Condamine in the northeastern corner of the Basin. He was educated at Toowoomba Grammar School and before entering politics ran an agribusiness. Mark Coulton, the member for Parkes, was the mayor of Gwydir, east of Moree, before entering federal politics, and is a grazier and farmer. Kevin Humphries, the NSW minister for natural resources, lands and water during the time of most of the allegations about poor compliance, was the National Party's member for Barwon, before the Shooters and Fishers' Roy Butler took the seat. Humphries grew up in Tamworth and was a schoolteacher in the area before running a management consultancy specialising in services to the cotton industry.

You will hear in the pubs of the Murray–Darling Basin that a few dominant families in the north are big donors to the National Party – though this is hard to substantiate on the material available from public sources. Rather, one is told about raffles – all properly licensed, but in which certain people buy most of the tickets. The influence is not only about money. It is a matter of worldview, of the tight bonds among people who built a successful industry of which they are proud.

Water users down south tend to perceive the National Party networks here as a seamless web of preference and influence. Up close, it clearly isn't that simple. I found no Joyce fans among the people in leadership positions in cotton country. In New South Wales there was a clear demarcation between the favoured few – the irrigators who have benefited most from government decisions – and the rest. And in Queensland there were plenty of critics of NSW Nationals, including successive state water ministers, for having been "asleep at the wheel" on protection of the environment and compliance. The cotton farmers I spoke to are sick of water politics. Frank Deshon is a Dirranbandi-based farmer and president of Smart Rivers, a lobby group for local water harvesters and irrigators. He described water politics as like being under attack by ants. "And that's okay for the bureaucrats. They get tired, they have a change of staff, and it's a nest – waves and waves of them coming after you and attacking you, and you can't not engage, or you lose any say." But he doesn't want the Basin Plan to fail. Now he is deeply engaged in the fish passages and the new measures to protect environmental water resulting from the Northern Basin review. The Plan, he says, is a start. It will have to be tweaked. But so many hours and so much money have been put into it. "We have to carry on."

Are the cotton farmers the enemy? They are certainly tired of being blamed for the problems of the Basin.

*

Tim Napier is the executive officer of Border Rivers Food & Fibre, which represents growers along the Dumaresq, Macintyre and Barwon rivers. We met over a coffee in Moree. Napier, of all the people I met, was the most reluctant to agree that there were systemic problems with compliance in the region. *Four Corners*? It was terrible. It had struck at their social licence to operate. His organisation had to withdraw from social media because of all the hostility. The South Australian royal commission he sees as having been called to "beat up New South Wales ... it became a honey pot for every individual or activist group who had an axe to grind." His organisation had taken the decision not to participate.

Napier rejects any suggestion that water theft is widespread, let alone to blame for the dry river downstream. "My comment is really, 'Where is the evidence to back up those claims?'" The legal system, he says, has a higher standard of proof than the media, and people are entitled to the presumption of innocence. But Napier is no defender of the NSW government's record. There have been, he says, "years of sub-standard administration and now the industry is taking the blame for their ineptitude." He said a lot more, too, about the attitudes that have made his members feel as though they are "under siege from urban-based activists who they see as applying different standards to themselves than they want to apply to others, in this case, farmers."

The farmers' point of view is best summed up by a joke on the Border Rivers Food & Fibre website. It is a spoof suggesting an urgent need for an "urban riparian restitution scheme" for city rivers, starting with the Tank Stream in Sydney – the key water source in colonial times but long since built over. "We, the Committee of Rural and Regional Australians and Zealots for the Environment, have decided this degradation, caused in no small part by millions of greedy Australians trying to earn a living each day, has to end … We apologise in advance for any inconvenience while we demolish the buildings of central Sydney so that one day the mighty, historic Tank Stream can flow once again."

The Queensland border town of Dirranbandi, population 639 – down almost 100 since Wong's water buybacks – is home to the famous Cubbie cotton station, the largest irrigation property in the Southern Hemisphere, nestled into the junction of the Balonne and Culgoa rivers and with the capacity to store the equivalent of Sydney Harbour in water. During the millennium drought, Cubbie got plenty of negative publicity. As the rivers dried up, it became the favoured target of those demonising cotton. Since then, Cubbie, now owned by the Chinese textile giant Shandong Ruyi and Macquarie Bank, has got better at public relations. A few months before my visit, the management put on tours for the media and for politicians and announced it would gift 10 gigalitres of water for environmental flows during dry periods.

Senator Patrick was on that tour and was impressed. In an area of country where metering of water can be slapdash and inconsistent, Cubbie knows to the millilitre what it has and where it has been used. Even those who disagree with the amount of water Cubbie takes from the system acknowledge that its licences have been legally acquired, its location is perfect and its management of water is "gold star" by world standards. The Cubbie method is to fill up the storages on a flood. That keeps the enterprise going through two or three years, during which lower flows from the rivers are also harvested. The business model is two to four years of maximum production, then three to four years of lower production, then two to three years of closing the operation down. It is the storages that allow Cubbie – and the other farmers who have built smaller Cubbies upstream – to gain some security and even out the booms and busts. One of the points of the Cubbie publicity tour was to try to make sure that this time around the drought would not be "about" Cubbie. The politicians and journalists were shown Cubbie's vast storages and 93,000 hectares of cotton fields. The storages were dry and the paddocks bare.

By the time I got there, the publicity drive was over and the board of Cubbie had decided they had appeased journalists enough. My request for a tour was declined, but I could see from the roads the huge, treeless black paddocks stretching to the horizon, devoid of vegetation. The Darling River was not to be found here.

Near Cubbie are the properties Kia Ora and Clyde, once owned by Eastern Australia Agriculture. *The Guardian*, in a long string of stories on water politics, has pursued the details of a deal cut during Joyce's time as minister, in which these properties were favoured for "strategic" water buybacks. They sold water to the Commonwealth for $79 million in a limited tender process, and after the water had previously been rejected twice. Eastern Australia Agriculture once included among its directors Liberal frontbencher Angus Taylor, now energy minister. He was no longer a director at the time of the sale and has said he had no involvement in the negotiations. This purchase, and others near here on the Warrego, have been criticised because they are for floodwater – known locally as "goanna water" because, in the words of Ed Fessey, "the only time you get it is when the goannas are sticking their heads out of the trees because of the flood."

Since the money was spent, there have been no flows against the licences bought from Clyde and Kia Ora – so no return on the taxpayer dollar. The Warrego licences yielded some water from Cyclone Trevor. Commonwealth Environmental Water Holder Jody Swirepik emphasised that her agency was not involved in the negotiations to buy water, but said she valued having the licences in her portfolio. Buying this kind of water licence was important. It meant that when the big rains came, the environment would have access to the "event" – to the boom time in the boom and bust rivers. Sometimes, she said, this was the only way to support sites such as the Narran Lakes.

I drove north to the town of St George – home of one of the origin stories of the cotton industry. The area was developed between the 1950s and '70s by the pro-development Bjelke-Petersen government, which built the Beardmore Dam on the Balonne to provide reliable water. The water was delivered by gravity through a system of channels. You can see why the cotton industry is close-knit by looking at the map of the irrigation scheme – 112 kilometres of channels and pipes spreading out in a dense network southeast of the town, like an elongated spider's web. It serves about fifty customers, mostly family businesses and mostly cotton, but also people who grow fodder – and the Moonrocks, a fifth-generation family farm that grows onions, broccoli and garlic for big supermarkets. Water metering is comparatively tight, and water theft from the irrigation system reputedly non-existent – certainly the system of metering would seem to make it impossible. You steal from the channel, and you are stealing not from some remote community downstream but from your neighbours and partners in the scheme. Some farmers also pump from the rivers, and tacitly acknowledge less confidence about their neighbours' compliance there.

People who demonise cotton farmers should meet Scott Armstrong, who is on the board of Mallawa Irrigation, which runs the St George irrigation scheme. He describes himself as "a part-time farmer and a full-time attender of water meetings," but he has largely given up engaging in water politics outside his local area, which he clearly loves. When it comes to state and national water politics, there is no point. "No matter what data you bring, the political animal just does its thing." Armstrong is impossible not to like – his pride in the St George irrigation area and his farm is evident in his every gesture. While we spoke, he drove his young son to a swimming lesson in the flat, bright town of St George, its prosperity unmistakeable even in these hard times. Then the two of them gave us a tour of the farm, the boy and his father clearly devoted to each other in that understated, wordless Aussie way. They were upset I had to see their farm when the land was dry. If only I had been there when it was in full production! But there were a few crops being grown here and in the farms roundabout – a bit of cotton, some pasture and some vegetables. I told them this was the healthiest farming country I had seen since I left Mildura, and Armstrong was surprised, and torn between pride and concern that I, "like most journalists," was really here to blame him and his community for the problems of the river.

He leant against a gantry over one of the irrigation channels and together we listened to the flow of water. They are still getting some – nothing like their usual allocation – thanks to the Beardmore Dam. "A beautiful sound," he said. "The best sound in the world for a farmer." "Once Australia was proud of people like me," he said. Now – he squinted at me – "the country and the city really don't understand each other, do they?"

For Armstrong, the history of water politics stretches far back – long before the Murray–Darling Basin Plan. The problems, he says, set in in 1989, when the state National Party government was in its dying days, and cotton was the equivalent of a goldrush and St George the centre of the success story. The state government decided there was enough water in the Beardmore Dam for extra entitlements. Armstrong recalls:

> We told them. We did all the modelling and we showed them that it was a very shallow dam and it wasn't a great idea to allocate more water out of it. And we said that doing so would kill the reliability of the scheme. And it didn't matter what data we showed them. They

> did it anyway. And they allocated extra out of a scheme that was already fairly well over-allocated. That was a National Party thing. And you know what was funny? Many of the new licences went to the well connected.

Since those times, there have been divisions in St George between the families who were there at the start of cotton prosperity and the beneficiaries of the later National Party largesse.

Soon after, in the early 1990s, the state government decided that anyone with a river frontage could harvest from it during floods. This was when Cubbie Station, among others, began to take off, treated favourably by state governments and overcoming legal challenges to its expansion. Says Armstrong, "We were sitting back and saying, 'It's all great in a wet year. But is this going to be long-term sustainable?' But it didn't matter what we argued. The regulators were happy, and so it happened." He holds no grudges against Cubbie. It has only done what the politicians have allowed it to do. It has acquired its licences legally and has developed them to the fullest extent allowed. He has done the same with his licences. Anybody would. But today, from Armstrong's point of view, St George is being blamed and forced to pay for the poor decisions of bureaucrats and politicians. "It doesn't matter how much we give up. Next time there is a change of government or a change of policy, there'll be another push, and another push. It's frustrating to see the erosion of the rights we thought we had as farmers."

The Basin Plan is just the latest example. Armstrong has arrived at a firm view on how water politics works: "Every time you hand over responsibility to a bunch of bureaucrats, it just seems to all end up in a big mess." But despite his complaints, he is proud of the fact that he and his neighbours have adapted. They will continue to adapt, he says. I asked him about climate change. The worst predictions for its impact on the Basin are apocalyptic. Armstrong is no climate change denier. But he stood a little straighter as he answered the question. "I can say I am confident that the

Australian farmer can adapt. It doesn't matter what the season throws at us. What the government throws at us. We'll make the best use of the resource, and deal with it, and we'll grow food and fibre for this nation and the world."

*

As we drove around cotton country, crisscrossing the border between New South Wales and Queensland, my travelling companion asked me who among those we had interviewed would be most unhappy with this essay. It was a good question. There had been a roar fit to shake the town in the front bar of the Dirranbandi pub when we told them I was a journalist writing about water. In Moree and Goondiwindi, some of the interviews had been hedged with suspicion and hostility. The cotton growers knew they were being blamed for the dry river downstream. They admitted little or no responsibility. Crop hating on crop, state hating on state. A society linked by water, but not a community. I replied that I thought everyone would be unhappy. That is the nature of the issue, of the failure of governance, dating back more than a century, that the Murray–Darling Basin represents.

The cotton growers of the north have, as Armstrong said of Cubbie, done what they have been allowed to do by governments and policymakers. So has everyone else, all along the river system. Some have got away with more than others for reasons of lobbying power, money, networks and geography. The result is a river system run to the edge of its ability to survive. If we are looking for the bad guys in this narrative, there are the water thieves, and possibly corrupt politicians and bureaucrats – the ICAC will tell us soon. But that is a small part of the story.

Blaming individuals, individual communities, or the growers of certain crops obscures the larger failure – of our politics when faced with a complex challenge. Underlying that is the failure of our ability, as Australians, to recognise common interests. But you can turn this around and call it a success, of a kind. That is what the bureaucrats who are implementing the

Plan prefer to do. They point out that it is extraordinary that the Murray–Darling Basin Plan exists at all. It is also why it is so hard to implement, to carry through the reform, and why success would be such an extraordinary achievement.

I drove on to the east, to look at the big private water storages that sprang up on the plains in a frenzy of dam-building, largely in the two years before allocations were capped about ten years ago. From the road, they don't look like much. If you didn't know what you were looking at, you could easily miss them. I stopped and committed a little trespass, scrambling up the sides. They are enormous. Vast swathes of country enclosed by walls a few metres high. When they are full, they are like mini-inland seas – "mini-Cubbies," the locals say, filling up the storages on the wet, eking it out through the dry. Some say Cubbie is dry now because of all the little Cubbies upstream. But the Darling wasn't there. All the storages were dry.

Finally, I drove up the rim of the Basin and into the Darling Downs, west of Brisbane. I walked through rainforests where it has not rained for many months. Some of them, between Warwick and Toowoomba, were on fire, the blazes not expected to go out for months. I came to Queen Mary Falls, in the headwaters of the Condamine River, and one of the beginnings – the twigs – of the Murray–Darling system. The advertisements for this tourist spot promise fragrant eucalypt forest, a creek plunging forty metres and "rainbows created by the waterfall's sheer mist." But Queen Mary Falls was little more than a dripping tap, and there were no rainbows.

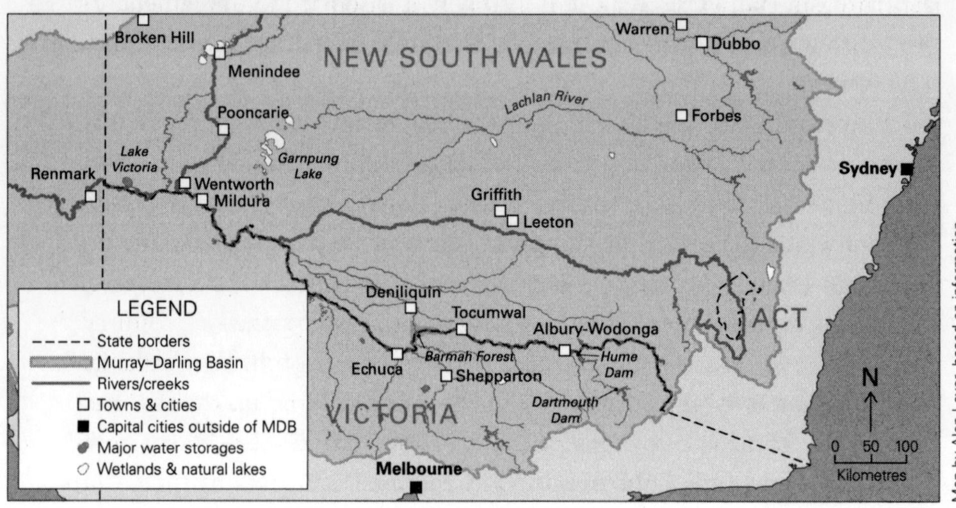

Map by Alan Laver, based on information from the Murray–Darling Basin Authority

National Party networks are the ones most under scrutiny in the Northern Basin, but in the last few years a new kind of political network has evolved around the Basin Plan and water politics. It is no reflection on the integrity of the actors to observe that they, too, have their networks – not always transparent. Here, politics is not operating as normal. The networks span the political spectrum, and unusual alliances have been formed.

Take, for example, the Australia Institute – the progressive think-tank headed by Ben Oquist, a friend and former chief of staff to the Greens' Bob Brown. The Australia Institute is usually associated with the environmental movement. The Murdoch press like to characterise it as the home of naive greenies, but it has never been that simple. For example, Oquist, a shrewd political strategist, has been crucial in influencing independent senator Jacqui Lambie, who has recruited some of her senior staff from the Australia Institute. He dealt with Clive Palmer, persuading him to block Tony Abbott's attempt to abolish the Clean Energy Finance Corporation.

More recently, the Australia Institute has reached deep into water politics through the work of its senior water researcher, Maryanne Slattery. Slattery is another former employee of the Murray–Darling Basin Authority turned critic. She worked at the Authority and its predecessor, the Murray–Darling Basin Commission, from 2005 until she left in 2017, dismayed by what she saw as the corruption of the Plan's implementation. Her last post was as director of environmental water policy. Since then, Slattery has become a whistleblower. She argues that a combination of poor execution and the water trading market has made the drought worse. She has written numerous reports, given evidence to the South Australian royal commission and been a source for most of the important pieces of journalism regarding the Plan (and for this essay). Slattery is shy and was initially not used to the bruising environment of public life. Now, though, she appears regularly in the media. She debated former water minister Littleproud on *Q&A* – formidably, because of her detailed understanding. She has a talent for making the complex understandable – something the bureaucrats at the Authority and the Water Holder often struggle to do. Some accuse her of oversimplification, but thanks to her work, more information is publicly available than would otherwise have been the case. She has made well-informed freedom-of-information requests and worked with senators Rex Patrick and Sarah Hanson-Young to force disclosures through Senate Committee hearings.

But in water politics, nothing is politically neutral. Slattery, like everybody else involved, comes from a particular point of view. She is hostile to the corporatisation of agriculture, and the big multinationals replacing family farms, and critical of the impact of water markets. Her job at the Australia Institute arose, she says, thanks to John Clements – former adviser to independent MP Tony Windsor, and now on the staff of NSW Shooters and Fishers MP Roy Butler – the man who, largely on the back of water politics, unseated the Nationals when he won the seat of Barwon in the 2019 NSW state election. Slattery says, "Clearly we don't agree on everything, but he respects integrity and honesty." When she left the Authority, Clements arranged philanthropic funding for her to take a short-term contract at the Australia Institute. She became one of its highest-profile employees.

Slattery's work is referred to by farmers throughout the Basin. Some are struggling to work out how it fits with the Australia Institute's presumed "greenie" tinge, but she is a household name from St George to Goolwa.

Slattery has worked particularly closely with another extraordinary political actor, an irrigator called Chris Brooks. He has been described in the pages of *The Australian* as probably the most effective political activist in Australia, outside capital cities. It is hard to argue with that assessment. Brooks and his networks have made politics-as-normal untenable in the Murray–Darling Basin. The result is driving a movement that threatens to bring the Basin Plan undone. Here the story shifts south, and east, to the other branch of the Basin tree – the reliable water powerhouses of the Murray and Murrumbidgee rivers and their tributaries, or the "tidy little river," as the northerners call it, with its forests of high-tech meters and comparatively steady flows from big public dams.

Brooks is a wealthy man. He was brought up on the family farm, near Barooga on the Murray near Tocumwal. He built a career as a grain trader when the Australian Wheat Board was having its last days as the monopoly marketer of Australian wheat. He hit the headlines as an important industry voice in the aftermath of the Iraqi wheat-for-oil scandal, in which kickbacks were paid to the regime of Saddam Hussein in contravention of UN sanctions. Later, he rose to be the CEO of Glencore, the giant global commodities trader, and duked it out at the highest levels of resource politics. In 2011, about the time the Gillard government was wheeling and dealing to legislate the Basin Plan, Brooks decided to semi-retire, returning to Barooga to grow wheat, canola and corn and raise lambs. It went well for a while. Then, as he puts it, "the Murray–Darling Basin Authority began to take away the water."

Brooks' house on the Barooga property rises above the plains around it. There are horses and well-kept gardens and, inside, a big room filled with the artefacts of his previous career and nods to the land that sustained it. Over the kitchen bench he has hosted politicians and farmers and wielded his power. Brooks is a forceful talker and an angry man. It is not hard to imagine that he might have found true retirement difficult. But these days he talks water all day long. When I interviewed him in late October 2019, Slattery was trying to reach him by phone. The previous night, *60 Minutes* had screened a program, "Water Rats," that had featured Brooks and resulted in a formal complaint of inaccuracy under the commercial television code of practice from the Murray–Darling Basin Authority. The program concerned allegations that the Authority had wasted millions of litres of water and caused environmental damage by flooding the Barmah-Millewa Forest, just downstream from Tocumwal. This is one of the allegations pushed by both Slattery and Brooks, and firmly believed by many of the locals. We'll get back to it.

The focus of Brooks' current fury is that he and his fellow southern NSW irrigators have this year had zero allocation against their general security water licences. Meanwhile, the farmers on the other side of the river, in Victoria, have an allocation. Brooks can see the river from his property, and there seems to be plenty of water flowing past, down towards South Australia and the almond trees near the border, and perhaps also for, as he puts it, "the bloody so-called environment, not that they manage that properly." But he isn't allowed to touch that water. Fresh from the paddocks, chowing down on a tin of tuna in between playing with his granddaughters, Brooks describes his own trajectory. He began out of frustration:

> In any business you have to deal with government, and normally you can work things out. But this Murray–Darling Basin Authority, there is no mediation. They have these community involvement processes, consulting ... they come along and they talk to a group about a particular issue and they want to block off this creek and all these stupid brainless concepts they come up with. And the locals

tell them it won't work. And they just go and do it anyway. It's a waste of water.

Around his home, where his family has farmed for four generations, is all the infrastructure of modern irrigation, such as the centre pivot sprinklers to spray water over the crops, the legacy of an era when governments encouraged farmers like his family to make the basin a food bowl. "And all of it closed down. Because someone turned the tap off," he said. He acknowledges there was once a surplus of water in the region, and much of it was sold to the Commonwealth during the Wong buybacks. But later, "What made me mad is these cunning, thieving, manipulative so-and-so's [buying water from] the government's National Party mates up north, and then the floodplain harvesting … the Angus Taylors and the Barnaby Joyces and all their friends were gutsing out on it … All of the National Party donors are in New South Wales, and they were the ones getting the floodplain harvesting, getting the deals on selling their water, going back and back to the trough." Meanwhile, he and his fellow Riverina farmers were seeing their allocations cut.

Brooks was not used to being ignored. "I got involved." He went to see Sussan Ley, the Liberal member for Farrer, which covers a large slab of the Riverina, its southern border running along the Murray from east of Albury to the South Australian border. "I told her to stand up for her constituents. And long story short, it didn't take too long to work out that she was part of the problem." Ley, he says, told him to go away, because he didn't represent anyone. Brooks decided to fix that. He stood successfully to become chair of the local irrigation council, and then of the Southern Riverina Irrigators, a coalition of five landholder associations. From this position, he drove a split in the statewide body, leaving the NSW Irrigators' Council because, he said, it didn't represent the interests of the south. In agricultural politics, this was seismic. "So I went back to Sussan with plenty of qualifications. I said, 'Lady, now you have an issue. You have to stop the National Party doing what it is doing to this area.' And we had some absolute stand-up ding-dong battles for six months. So I said, 'Okay, we are going to kick you out.'"

In the March 2019 NSW state election, Brooks managed and financed the campaign of Shooters and Fishers candidate Helen Dalton, who took the seat of Murray from the Nationals with a massive 26 per cent swing. It was her third attempt, but her first success. Most of the farmers who backed Dalton had voted National all their lives. No longer. How did the Shooters, Fishers and Farmers Party address their needs? The party's platform is couched in words such as freedom and rights: "The right to farm free from oppressive green and red tape," for example. But when it comes to NSW policy, water management is first and foremost. The party's platform states that the Murray–Darling Basin Plan has "failed farmers." It calls for uniform high-quality metering, an audit of water and a federal royal commission into the Murray–Darling Basin Plan. In other words, it adopts the agenda of the farmers of the Southern Basin, over that of the north. The farmers of Farrer widely believe that such a royal commission, if it ever takes place, has the potential to bring the National Party undone.

Brooks wasn't finished. Attempting to deliver on his threat to Ley, he and his followers founded a new party, Voices for Farrer, which backed the campaign of Kevin Mack, former mayor of Albury, to run against Ley in the 2019 federal election. Mack was a dream candidate – previously approached by One Nation, Clive Palmer and the National Party. But although most commentators rated him a strong chance, he lost. Says Brooks: "We gave it a good run, but long story short we just got rolled. It was nothing to do with Ley. It was because people were frightened of Bill Shorten." Mack achieved a 10 per cent swing against Ley, who holds one of the safest federal Liberal seats.

Brooks' disgust grew when Ley was made environment minister after the election. The Southern Riverina Irrigators commissioned research from Maryanne Slattery. Her "very accurate facts," says Brooks, enabled the group to keep up the pressure. In particular, Slattery's research has formed the basis of a class action in which the Southern Riverina Irrigators are suing the Murray–Darling Basin Authority, using an analysis of the Authority's own flow data.

According to Brooks, he first considered taking action under the constitution – challenging the basis of Commonwealth power over water. The legal advice was that they could spend a lot of money with no certainty of result. In the end, they decided to take a common law action. It is a serious business, financed by a litigation funder and with senior legal council. And here the branches of the tree that is the Murray–Darling Basin connect in a narrative, because part of the claim is about the management of the Menindee Lakes.

The claim relates to the 2016 draining of the Menindee Lakes, despite it being a relatively wet year in South Australia. As a result of this, when the drought began there were no reserves and hence no flows from the Darling. When the Darling stopped flowing, the burden of supplying South Australia fell entirely on the Murray and its tributaries – Victoria and the irrigators of southern New South Wales. The Southern Riverina Irrigators' statement of claim goes on to allege that the Authority then failed, when it could have done so, to fill the storages of Lake Victoria, a major storage near the South Australian border, in subsequent years. That meant that, in the 2018/19 summer, there was a rush to force water downstream – at "hideous levels," in Brooks' words, losing 6200 megalitres a day to overbank flows, and flooding the Barmah Forest. All this, the statement of claim says, is "gross negligence" and the reason Brooks and his fellows have been watching crops die as water flows past their properties. They are seeking damages of $750 million.

From his bailiwick in Barooga, Brooks' hostile gaze falls upstream, on the National Party networks of the north, and downstream, on the almond growers, South Australia and the management of the lower lakes. The political campaign continues. Brooks has said he will help fund a welter of independents and minor-party candidates at federal and state elections. He has threatened to try to unseat the Nationals' Anne Webster and

Damian Drum in the Victorian seats of Mallee and Nicholls. He says he will take on Deputy Prime Minister Michael McCormack in the NSW seat of Riverina and, again, Sussan Ley in Farrer. Brooks' charisma, his success in drawing farmers to the cause, his use of Slattery's research, his ability to tap the growing desperation of drought-hit farmers and the perception that the National Party takes care only of its Northern Basin mates has made the politics close to unmanageable. Meanwhile, he peppers NSW politicians with letters, and increasingly they seem to dance to his tune.

Phillip Glyde, chief executive of the Authority, like a good public servant is reluctant to comment on the politics, but between the lines of his careful statements two things emerge: first, frustration and dismay at the NSW government – its early history of poor policing of compliance, its failure to complete water management plans on time, its constant threats to pull out of the Plan – which he acknowledges would be a "disaster." But mixed with this is an apparent sympathy for the governments, federal and state, in dealing with politics gone feral. "It's hard for [New South Wales] to move forward on the Basin Plan, when you've got people like Chris Brooks jumping up and down."

The longer the drought goes on, the harder the politics become.

*

Meanwhile, the politics, the policy and the management collide, once again, with the realities of landscape – in this case, an area the water engineers refer to as the Barmah Choke. Language contains within it the habits of thought, telling you a lot about attitudes. The locals have a gentler name for this part of the Murray. They call it the Narrows. Here, in a redgum forest between Tocumwal and Echuca, all the narratives of nature, history, markets, land and politics compete. The Narrows, or the Choke, is in fact three spots – one at Tocumwal, one in the Barmah-Millewa Forest and one where the Edward river meets the Murray. The Edward Choke is at Picnic Point, a spot many tourists to the Riverina have probably visited. A fragrant eucalypt forest clothes the banks. There is a caravan park and barbecues, and waterskiers ply up and down. The names round here are evocative: Poverty Point Road, but also Bunyip Trek and Cornucopia Road.

Before and after the Narrows, the Murray can sprawl magnificently, its width challenging a swimmer. At the Choke, you can stand on one bank of the mighty Murray and imagine easily lobbing a rock or a branch to the other side. The Narrows are the result of an uplift of land along a faultline near Deniliquin 25,000 years ago. Every year, as the spring snow melt made its way down, the river would break its banks and flood. As a result, the Barmah–Millewa river redgum forest – an internationally important wetland – formed over the centuries. Today it is a national park. For the river managers, the Choke is a problem. It divides the river. Only around 7000 megalitres a day can get through here without bursting the bank. The Choke restricts water trading downstream of Cobram and upstream of Echuca. When the water traders have the stuff for sale, they reference it as above Choke, or below.

Part of the Southern Riverina Irrigators' claim, and a firm belief among the local farmers I met in the Riverina, is that the Commonwealth Environmental Water Holder and the Basin Authority are flooding the Barmah Forest too often, all in the rush to get water to the almonds and South Australia. In the spring and summer of 2018/19, Lake Victoria was not as full as it needed to be for the irrigation season. In the words of the Authority, "overbank transfers from Hume Dam became a necessity to appropriately manage the risk of a delivery shortfall in the months ahead." More water than usual was lost in "conveyance," partly because of the heat and greater evaporation, and partly because of the water breaching the banks and seeping in. Commonwealth Environmental Water Holder Jody Swirepik says the need to get water downstream to meet irrigation orders affected the ability to meet the needs of the environment. The entire capacity of the river was needed to carry irrigation water. It could not carry environmental water as well. Creeks and wetlands downstream missed out on their environmental springtime drink. At the same time, the extra irrigation water going downstream extended the time that the Barmah Forest was partly flooded.

I went to the sites of alleged damage. To my admittedly inexpert eye, it wasn't obvious. The locals told me that the Water Holder is flooding the forest more often than is natural, harming trees and wasting water. They talk about how the Barmah Forest was in their childhoods, or when their parents used to play there all year long. Back then, the forest would flood only one year in five, they say. To them, the more frequent environmental flows are vandalism – a departure from the natural. But Swirepik says the water that has flowed into the Hume and Dartmouth dams upstream demonstrates that if there were no dams, and no irrigation extraction, there would have been high flows through the Choke in the spring of 2018, despite the drought. In its natural state, the forest would have flooded in nineteen of the last twenty years. "Local people find it hard to believe, because the living memory is after the Hume was built so people don't necessarily have an appreciation of what it might have been like before."

Some locals claim the forest is suffering, because it is not as they remember it. This is taken as proof that the environment is being given too much water, and that the Canberra bureaucracy "hasn't a clue" how to manage it. Swirepik says the Barmah-Millewa Forest is in better shape than it has been for generations; it is one of the healthiest sites in the whole system and one of the success stories of the Murray–Darling Basin Plan. The two sides could be talking about different rivers. They are certainly talking about different ideas of the natural.

There is one area of agreement between the Canberra bureaucrats and the locals. Everyone is worried about what the new almond plantations downstream mean for the future, when they reach maturity and the growers demand water every year. Glyde admits he is "very concerned" about whether there is enough water in the system for those trees when they reach maturity, but also about whether the Authority would be able to deliver it – including through the Choke. I put it to him that the free marketeers would say this is a risk that almond growers should factor in. Let the market sort it out. Glyde responds that this assumes the market is perfect and everyone has equal access to information. He says history suggests people make investments on advice, and when it comes to water the advice isn't always right. "People sold their water in 2012 on advice, when it started to rain. They were told it was in their economic interest, and that they would be able to buy the water back on the temporary market. That worked really well for a couple of years. But others said, 'It's going to get dry again,' and hung on to their water." Now, the price of water is sky-high – driven in part by the almond plantations, and many of the growers who sold their water are on their knees. "So there was either bad decision-making or poor information given."

Glyde believes there is a lot of work to be done to improve the markets. He looks forward to the report of the current ACCC inquiry. In the meantime, he points out: the costs of missteps won't be borne only by the investors in almond plantations. If the industry goes bad, the communities involved will pay, and by extension the rest of Australia.

Glyde doesn't say it, but if in some future world almond trees die because the Authority can't deliver water, Brooks and his fellow litigants won't be the only people likely to sue the government.

*

I drove north from Barooga, on to the Hay Plains. Curtains of rain – not enough to be drought-breaking, the locals assured me – swept across the sky and the soil glowed orange. The road is ruler-straight, except for the occasional curve that seems to have been designed to get sleepy drivers off the road. And there they are: big, new earthen-banked water storages, resembling those in the Northern Basin. Some of them, at least, have been funded with the money handed out by the federal government for efficiency schemes. In 2019, Slattery responded to claims by ministers that new dams were not being built in Australia. They were, she said – but they were private dams, part-funded by public money. Slattery and Senator Rex

Patrick, working together, tried to get information on how much taxpayer money was in those dams. They were not entirely successful, but she estimated that two of them received nearly $30 million, while dam-related projects in the wider Murray–Darling had received over $200 million.

The justification for the dams, from an efficiency point of view, is that they allow for use of recycled, stored water. Or the money might be used to deepen an existing dam, thus limiting evaporation losses. Slattery counters that if evaporation is a concern, it would be better to store the water in the big public dams. She suggests that the dams store "supplementary water" – the flows that come in a wet year, which previously would have flowed into the rivers and to groundwater. "Supplementary flows make up almost all the water that has historically gone from the Murrumbidgee into the Murray. With major dams now targeting this water, the Murrumbidgee could be disconnected from the Murray in most years."

Thanks to Slattery, the Hay Plain dams have had a fair bit of media attention. They are one of the most visible examples of government-funded efficiency schemes on private land. Since Joyce capped water buybacks, these have been the main way of clawing back water for the environment. The spending is controversial for a number of reasons. First, according to the Productivity Commission, it is twice as expensive as simply purchasing the same amount of water. The rationale for ladling out the taxpayer dollar in this way is that it helps farmers and minimises the impact on regional communities of reduced water use – avoiding the so-called Swiss cheese effect of water buybacks. The Productivity Commission has been sceptical about that argument. Water buybacks are not the main cause of structural change in regional towns, it has said – but they do tend to get blamed for the declines in jobs and population. Another reason for the controversy is that the money flows into private hands, with little transparency around who gets funding and why. Sometimes the taxpayer is paying for things that the growers might have done on their own had the grants not been available. The Productivity Commission has said not all schemes have given value for money.

A more serious concern is that the government chequebook, together with the water trading system, is changing the Basin in unintended ways – possibly contributing to high water prices and future management problems. The new dams on the Hay Plains, and many of the almond plantations they support, are an example of this. They are greenfield investments – irrigation infrastructure where none has been before. Given that the diversions from the river are capped, how can this be so?

David Pearce, of the Centre for International Economics, remarks that it is a well-understood principle of economics that if you make an activity more efficient, you may increase that activity. He gives an analogy. If you become more energy-efficient and reduce your electricity bill, you are unlikely to put the saved money in the bank. Rather, you may buy a flatscreen television – which uses more energy. So irrigators who have received taxpayer money to help them use water more efficiently are then more likely to buy water on the open market, make efficient use of it and expand their operations. The only thing that prevents this expanding in an unlimited fashion is a cap – and the Murray–Darling Basin is meant to have such a cap in the sustainable diversion limit, both Basin-wide and in each area.

But the cap doesn't really work like that. It's a big-picture, macro measure, not a description of what happens in any particular place at any particular time. It is based on long-term averages. The amount of water actually used varies from season to season, affected by weather, water trading and the carrying forward of entitlements from previous years.

Professor Quentin Grafton, a water economist at the ANU Crawford School of Public Policy, argues that the only way to manage the river properly is at a fine-grained, local level – and that the knowledge needed to do this is lacking. He has raised a fundamental issue – one that could, if the most pessimistic estimates are right, undermine the entirety of the Murray–Darling Basin Plan. It is the main reason he and other academics have described the management of the river as having entered "a post-truth world." If Grafton and his colleagues are right, the amount of water clawed back for the environment, and now managed by the Commonwealth Environmental Water Holder, might have been partly or entirely cancelled out by the effect of the so-called efficiency schemes.

It works like this. When irrigators use water less efficiently, not all of it is consumed by crops. Some of it seeps back into the soil and ultimately makes its way to aquifers or back to the rivers and streams. This is called the "return flow." Efficiency measures can include things such as drip irrigation or the use of soil moisture meters that shut off watering once the root zone is saturated. That reduces or even eliminates the return flow. Grafton gives an example. An increasingly common water trade in recent years has been for growers of irrigated pasture in Victoria to trade water 1200 kilometres to the west, to almond growers on both sides of the South Australian border. The pasture grower would have been using overhead sprinklers, meaning there would be return flows. The South Australian nut grower would use drip irrigation, precisely measuring how much each tree needed. Little or nothing would return to the river. "That difference," says Grafton, "would not be included in the trade, because the trade is based on gross diversions – not net water use. So what that means is that you can easily get increases in water consumption in the system that we don't count, and that's even if the system is well monitored and managed and all that other stuff."

Nobody is denying that Grafton has a point. The question is, how big is the loss to the river system from greater efficiency? Grafton claims that when he first raised the issue with the Authority, he was told it was not a priority because the amounts involved would be "negligible." In response, he and his colleague John Williams did some modelling. They came up with some very large figures. On a worst-case scenario, environmental flows under the Plan might actually have *reduced* by a net 140 gigalitres a year – the reduction in return flows more than cancelling out the water recovered for the environment. In the best-case scenario, stream flows would have increased by only 280 gigalitres a year – well below the 700 gigalitres a year the government is claiming to have recovered from water efficiency subsidies. Grafton admits there is considerable uncertainty in their estimates.

After Grafton's work, the Authority commissioned another study. That came back with different, less alarming figures. The net reduction, it suggested, was just 121 gigalitres a year. It was still a considerable amount of water.

The truth, as Grafton acknowledges, is nobody really knows the scale of the problem. Because of this and all the other uncertainties – floodplain harvesting, water theft issues and so on – he believes there should be a comprehensive water audit, at the level of the individual irrigation property. It would cost millions of dollars, and several years of data would be needed. It would mean at least a pause in the implementation of water recovery by subsidies for irrigation efficiency projects.

The political reality is that irrigator peak bodies and state governments are strongly against pausing infrastructure subsidies. Some irrigators also oppose a detailed water audit – apparently fearing it may result in more water being claimed back from them. Glyde admits there is "definitely an issue to watch" with return flows, but the modelling so far suggests "it is not an issue sufficient to change the fundamentals of the Plan." But he acknowledges that if it is discovered that the Plan has underestimated the return flows issue, then "we'll have to deal with it." In this, Glyde does not so much disagree with his critics, as disagree with the implications of what they say. What they call a "post-truth world" he sees as an inevitable part of a natural resource management plan. Such a plan, he says, is always full of uncertainties. One must plan, review and adjust.

All that is complicated by the need to maintain the political compact. The efficiency spending – the doling out of taxpayer money to growers – is one way of maintaining the fragile compact among the jurisdictions that are the subject of the experiment.

*

In September 2019 near Tocumwal, there was an act of vandalism. Gravel and rocks were dumped into an irrigation channel used to release environmental water into the Barmah Forest. It was a hint that some of the talk of terrorism might actually come to pass. The ABC's *Country Hour* quoted Chris Brooks saying, "Desperate men do desperate things. I see the look in people's faces and they are pretty angry. It worries me, but it is going to happen." He said he had nothing to do with the vandalism and did not condone it. A week earlier, there had been a protest in Tocumwal. An effigy of Littleproud had been floated into the river and headed towards South Australia, armed with a tracking device and signs asking people who saw it to take photos and report back. The Tocumwal rally organiser, Lindsay Schultz, said: "We're trying to get through to people how much water is actually going down this river, into the lower lakes and out into the sea, that could be used for growing food for our nation."

A meeting of the Ministerial Council was due in December, and in the lead-up New South Wales was once again threatening to withdraw from the Basin Plan. Littleproud was fully engaged in trying to keep the Plan intact, the show on the road – not least by appeasing Brooks and his supporters. In January 2019, the Productivity Commission had recommended that the Authority be split into two and compliance matters be given to a new agency. The Authority could not work with the states and simultaneously be expected to effectively monitor their compliance, it said.

The government rejected the idea of a new body, but instead established a new position, Interim Inspector-General of Murray–Darling Basin Water Resources, billed by Littleproud as a "top cop" for the Basin. Littleproud appointed Mick Keelty, the former head of the Australian Federal Police. Keelty already held the position of Northern Basin Commissioner – part of the federal government's response to the *Four Corners* revelations. With this appointment, Keelty began a process not so much of mission creep, but mission gallop.

His appointment as "top cop" was announced in August 2019. I was travelling in the Basin. Most of the people I spoke to were pleased and took his appointment as a sign the government would sort out compliance issues. Keelty has great credibility in the bush. He presented himself to the media, and to Senate Estimates hearings, as a plain-speaking man of action in a maze of scientists, engineers and bureaucrats. Senators, perhaps glazed from the technicalities of water management, loved him. In media interviews, Keelty talked a tough game. The complexity of water-licensing arrangements across the Basin created a climate for corruption, he said. He talked about making water licensing uniform – just as state agreements had led to uniformity in the rules of the road.

Keelty's tough talk doubtless helped Littleproud manage the politics, but the word "interim" in Keelty's title was a sign of trouble to come. Littleproud needed the approval of the states to give Keelty investigative powers. That relied on the approaching Ministerial Council meeting.

In early December, Chris Brooks led a demonstration to Canberra under the slogan "Can the Plan." There were buses of protesters, about 1000 people in all, and close to 100 trucks. They did laps of Parliament House, slowing traffic, with slogans describing the Basin Plan as an "unnatural disaster." Brooks addressed the rally early in the day, and then was called in as part of a delegation for a personal chat with Littleproud. Keelty was there. Apparently on the spot, Littleproud promised to give Keelty a new role: to investigate the water-sharing agreement among the states. The announcement came as a complete surprise to Glyde, the head of the Murray–Darling Basin Authority. He says he was given no warning.

Was this policy-making on the run – a sop to Brooks and the NSW government? Glyde naturally won't comment, but says he thinks there is merit in the idea of reviewing the states' water sharing – but that is for the states to do, not the Authority. Is Keelty the right man for the job? Easy to understand a former top cop being given a role in compliance. Harder to see why he is the right person for reviewing a water-sharing agreement that dates back to federation. To add to the difficulties, the job is meant to be completed by March 2020.

Whatever the thinking, Brooks was clearly pleased. He came out to his supporters in front of Parliament House and presented it as a "huge win" and a backflip by the government. The idea quickly got around – and some say it is Brooks who has encouraged its spread – that Littleproud had effectively promised the Southern Basin irrigators that Keelty's review would mean they would get more water in time for the autumn irrigation season. It's easy to see how that idea took hold, even though Brooks has never quite said it. One of the Can the Plan organisers, Darcy Hare, who does research for Brooks, said the Keelty review would allow him to "to find buckets of water that are locked away and not utilised due to archaic rules which could provide relief to farmers and communities." Brooks' published statements stop short of this, but after meetings with Keelty in January 2020, he said: "We have turned the corner; the future is looking brighter. I am hoping we now get a better and fairer allocation of water in the new irrigation season."

Keelty, while continually emphasising that he is politically independent, lauded Littleproud's leadership in facing the protesters.

Glyde has also heard the suggestion that the Keelty review will translate into more water for Brooks and his supporters. He can't see how that can be right. There is simply no new water in the system. If the southern irrigators are to get more, somebody else will have to give it up. How can that be done? Perhaps the South Australian desalination plant could provide more water for Adelaide, freeing up a bit – but it wouldn't be much, and it would be expensive.

When the Ministerial Council met just before Christmas 2019, New South Wales did not leave the Basin Plan – although by now this was almost a technical distinction, because New South Wales also made it clear that it had no intention of fulfilling its obligations. It would not bring forward the water resource plans. It would not contribute to the 450 gigalitres of agreed extra environmental flow. The communiqué from the meeting bristled with unresolved issues. It "noted" Keelty's new role but did not grant him the powers Littleproud had requested: "Some State Ministers expressed concern that the investigation extends to a review of water sharing arrangements and that they will not participate. The Commonwealth Minister confirmed the investigation will commence immediately."

In January 2020, I was hearing reports from Keelty's tour of the Basin – yet another inquiry hitting the road. Typically, he asks for constructive ideas to take back to Canberra. He tells people he is not interested in hearing gripes. He also makes it clear that he is getting absolutely no cooperation from state governments. He told a meeting in Deniliquin that he had never seen a group so divided as the country's water ministers.

Chris Brooks was at that meeting. He charged Keelty with taking a message back to Littleproud. "The financial and mental stress on people of this region, brought about by this mismanagement, will not be tolerated any longer, and there will be retribution if it is ignored," he said. "And that's not a threat. That is an absolute promise."

So has Brooks been made a promise of more water? Littleproud denies it, but at the very least he was leaning heavily on Keelty's credibility. The crunch will come when Keelty reports, in March. Littleproud won't be there to deal with it. In February 2020, as this essay was being written, the scandal over the sports rorts affair and a challenge by Barnaby Joyce for the National Party leadership led to a ministerial reshuffle. Littleproud lost the water portfolio and became minister for agriculture. He is often talked of as the heir apparent to National Party leader Michael McCormack.

Political commentators described the water portfolio as a "poisoned chalice" – surely an understatement. Littleproud had committed to the Plan – unlike his predecessor, Joyce. He had done his best to keep the political compact hanging together. But the job was only going to get more difficult and contentious – not ideal for an ambitious leader in waiting.

Littleproud's replacement as water minister is Keith Pitt, a former sugarcane farmer representing the electorate of Hinkler on the Queensland coast – which is outside the Basin. He also gained the Resources portfolio. Pitt is best known for resigning as an assistant minister in 2018 in protest at the government committing to reduce greenhouse gas emissions, and for supporting new coalmines and nuclear energy. He is generally seen as a supporter of McCormack against Joyce. His first public statements in his new role were to call for more coal, uranium and gas exports. The Can the Plan activists were not happy. In an interview with the Deniliquin local paper as this essay went to print, one of the protest organisers said they had been at last making progress with Littleproud, and suspected Pitt's appointment was an attempt to get rid of him so as to "further stall any efforts to fix the basin plan." Another convoy to Canberra was on the cards.

Back in Barooga, it is quite clear where Brooks and his supporters think extra water is to be found, and why they see the water-sharing agreement between the states as an answer to their woes. They have their eyes on South Australia's guaranteed 1850 gigalitre allowance, and the management of the lower lakes.

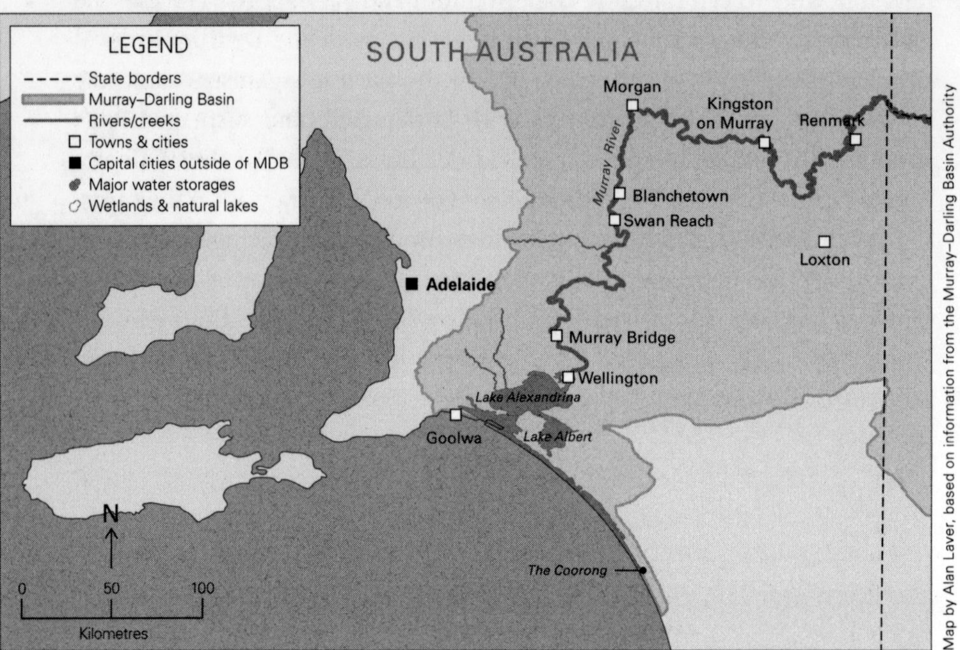

Map by Alan Laver, based on information from the Murray–Darling Basin Authority

The effigy of David Littleproud that the Can the Plan protesters put into the river in September 2019 at Tocumwal was sighted later that month in Echuca. People hauled Littleproud onto their houseboat, took a picture and posted it to Facebook. The minister for water was looking the worse for wear. He was travelling towards the Murray Mouth at a rate of 12 kilometres a day, with 1718 kilometres to go. Someone was clearly refurbishing him as he went. He had acquired glasses, and a suit. In October, he was fished out further downstream, and taken for a drive around Nyah, north of Swan Hill, and particularly the Vinifera State Forest, where the locals claim environmental watering has killed trees and bred populations of European carp. The Victorian Environmental Water Holder, meanwhile, claims the watering has been "particularly successful," with swamp wallabies returning and frogs, birds and small fish reviving. As with the Barmah Forest, they could be talking about different places. Given the number of snags, locks and weirs, Littleproud probably won't make it to the Murray Mouth, and since the real Littleproud managed to appease Chris Brooks and his supporters, the protesters have been less vocal about tracking the effigy's progress. Nor have there, at the time of writing, been any effigies created of his replacement, Keith Pitt.

If some fraction of the Littleproud effigy remains, it might now be reaching the trunk of the tree of the Murray–Darling Basin system in South Australia. In this, the driest state in the driest country in the world, the river runs a murky green through semi-desert country, hedged by sandstone cliffs and, on the bends, spreading out into billabongs and wetlands. Hugging the curves of the river are some of the oldest irrigation settlements in the country. Built on the reliable water of South Australia's agreed share, almost all the crops are permanent – fruit and nut trees and grapevines.

I was brought up in Adelaide. My weekends and holidays were spent in the Riverland. As a child, in the 1960s and '70s, I remember playing in open irrigation channels when the water flowed. The horizons were wreathed in spray from overhead sprinklers. By the time I was a teenager, all that had changed. The irrigators, largely at their own expense, installed similar "efficiency measures" to those that are now being funded with federal money upstream. Open channels became pipes. Sprinklers were replaced with drip irrigation. The South Australian government capped extractions from the Murray in 1969, well ahead of other states. All this meant that when the call for further savings was made as part of the lead-up to the Basin Plan, South Australia had less left to do than the upstream growers. Nevertheless, this region has given up 10.8 gigalitres to the Commonwealth as a result of buybacks and efficiency schemes.

South Australia gets its guaranteed 1850 gigalitres in recognition that by the time the river reaches the border, there are no more tributaries adding to its water. If the river is to run, if the salt in the system is to be flushed to the sea, if South Australian irrigators are to be able to run their businesses and Adelaide is to have enough water, then South Australia must have its share of the inflows from upstream. Usually, the 1850 gigalitres is a guaranteed minimum – in a wet year, there will be more. In a dry year, it might be reduced.

Most of the time when you talk to the water managers of the Basin, you get the impression the river ends at the South Australian border. All the emphasis is on getting that 1850 gigalitres over the line, in accord with the agreements struck by the states, dating back to federation. From there, South Australia, sitting at the end of the long chain of dysfunction, has been largely left to run its own race. That may be about to change.

The Renmark Irrigation Trust presiding member, Humphrey Howie, sympathises with the Southern Riverina Irrigators. During the millennium drought, normal state water-sharing arrangements were suspended. South Australian Riverland irrigators were told they would get as little as 4 per cent of their licensed allocations, and the board of the trust was rolled in a wave of grower anger. But, says Howie, the South Australians learnt from the experience. The Irrigation Trust restructured, and the water allocations within the state were reorganised. Thanks to a new desalination plant, Adelaide reduced its reliance on the Murray, to make more water available for irrigators in dry years. South Australia, says Howie, has done the right thing.

In late January, Mick Keelty visited Renmark. On the eve of the planned public meeting, Howie told the local paper he didn't see how South Australia could get much benefit out of his inquiry. It was, he said, the result of Littleproud having to give the Can the Plan protesters something. "He probably didn't want to do it, but he's stuck with it." And in the wake of the Keelty meeting, Howie told me he had no clearer view of what might result. It was now an inquiry into state agreements without the backing of the states.

Howie and his fellow irrigators are nervous. They know that hungry eyes are turned downstream, and the relative security of South Australia's water looks, to many, like a luxury. They have the same refrain, for different reasons, as the irrigators of the Northern Basin. People elsewhere just don't understand. Being closer to the mouth, *we* understand what will happen if water is withdrawn and the river mouth closes. The Murray drains through land that once, centuries ago, was under sea. It picks up salt on its travels. If water isn't flushed through the mouth, that salt will back up, further and further up the system. Rivers, they say in South Australia, die from the mouth. Upstream, they say that water sent to the sea is "waste."

The particular focus of those hoping to get some of South Australia's allocation is the water that is "lost" to the sun and air. It is estimated that evaporation in South Australia accounts for between a third and half of the 1850 gigalitre allowance. Most of the evaporation happens in the lower lakes – Lake Alexandrina and Lake Albert – sheets of water so large they feel like the sea. Together the lakes total over 800 square kilometres of water. The river enters Lake Alexandrina at the town of Wellington. Most of the river's flow used to pass through the channel between Hindmarsh Island and Goolwa, before exiting to the sea. Now, thanks to five barrages built across the mouth in the 1880s to keep seawater back and protect irrigation, the flow into the sea is managed. The claim by those with eyes on those evaporation losses is that the lower lakes should be opened to the sea, the barrages either demolished or managed differently, and a new lock – lock zero – installed at Wellington to hold back saltwater. The implication is that South Australia's allocation could then be cut by at least the amount of the saved evaporation losses.

Brooks talks of the lower lakes and their management with contempt. He sees the listing of the Coorong as internationally protected Ramsar wetlands as a hoax, built on a lie. Fuelling this is an academic dispute surrounding the work of Professor Peter Gell, currently professor of environmental science at Federation University, but formerly at the University of Adelaide. Gell's work is being talked about right along the Murray and Murrumbidgee. People one would not normally expect to be reading academic journal articles made me promise to read it. His assertions have been picked up by the Institute of Public Affairs and used to discredit the

Murray–Darling Basin Plan and the Commonwealth *Water Act*. The independent member for Shepparton, Suzanna Sheed, has called on the Victorian government to "vigorously investigate" Gell's claims. "What now appears to be the case is that the whole of the Murray–Darling Basin Plan was based on incorrect science provided by South Australia."

As is so often the case in the claustrophobic academic circles of Adelaide, it all began on North Terrace, the centre of South Australia's academic and university community. In 2007, Gell published a paper with colleagues, including two postdoctoral researchers, John Tibby and Jennie Fluin, based on an analysis of cores of mud drawn from the lower lakes. They were looking at diatoms – single-celled algae – over time and what they could reveal about the lower lakes environment before European settlement. The resulting co-authored paper was published without controversy in 2007. Its main findings concerned the evolution of Lake Alexandrina and Lake Albert. After that, relations between Tibby, Fluin and Gell grew strained over academic disputes of no relevance to this essay. Gell moved on to Federation University. Then, in 2019, there was a bombshell. Gell published another paper, drawing on the same data and effectively accusing Fluin in particular of distorting information to support the Murray–Darling Basin Plan. The paper was published by the CSIRO, and later withdrawn and some corrections made – the editor emphasises there was no suggestion of academic misconduct. Nevertheless, the message was clear. Gell was asserting that the attempt to maintain the freshwater nature of the lower lakes was based on false science. In fact, he said, the diatoms indicated the lakes had been estuarine, and largely salt. Gell effectively accused the South Australian government and his fellow academics of misleading the public. The result, he claimed, underpinned the whole Plan and the decision, made way back in 2012, to claw back 2750 gigalitres a year for the environment.

John Tibby disputes Gell's interpretation of the data and is clearly furious at the allegations of academic misconduct. The debate is impossibly technical for a general reader, but to sum it up, Tibby argues that the diatoms discussed by Gell don't necessarily mean a predominantly marine environment. The creatures could have lived in both fresh and saltwater environments. And, he says, not a line of his and Fluin's work was used to justify the international listing of the lower lakes. "I would be proud if it was, but it wasn't." The balance of the admittedly incomplete evidence, he says, is that the lakes were mostly freshwater, with variations depending on the season and the river flow. If a decision were made to build a lock zero and return the lower lakes to saltwater, it would create an ecosystem that has no precedent in history.

Ben Bruce, the chief executive of the South Australian Department of Environment, Water and Natural Resources, regards Gell's work as, at best, "one of the inputs" on the pre-settlement nature of the lakes, to be weighed against other evidence. Most scientists think the lower lakes were mainly fresh, drawing on all kinds of evidence – early records, the flora and the fauna. Gell is an outlier – in the minority. The case for lock zero is flawed, he says, and based on a misunderstanding. Building a lock at Wellington would be close to impossible due to centuries of silt. Even if it was possible, the water held behind the lock would supply Adelaide and South Australian country towns. Water quality would have to be maintained – salt flushed and blue-green algae prevented. The amount of water needed to do that flushing would negate any savings. As well as this, he says, allowing seawater into the lower lakes would fundamentally change the nature of the protected wetland. Opening the barrages would therefore be a breach of Australian law.

Bruce and his department have been saying these things for a while but, he acknowledges, it has made almost no impact on the debate. He asked me for hints on how to get the message across.

The promotion of Gell's work continues. He has been written up uncritically in the rural press with the suggestion that his work is revelatory, rather than disputed. And, like most political problems concerning the Murray–Darling Basin, the controversy has sparked an independent review of "the science of the lower lakes," which will report later this year.

You can have strange, sad conversations on the Murray–Darling. I met an irrigator who was going broke. He exemplified the dilemma of the angst of farmers in a nation that no longer understands them. He did it tough through the millennial drought, and by the time Penny Wong was buying water, he was burdened by debt. He took financial advice and sold some of his water and was able to carry on. He shifted partly into dryland farming, and partly into growing fruit trees. Now, he has no water allocation, and he can't afford to outbid the water barons to buy enough to keep the trees alive. He is trying to reimagine himself as not being a farmer. There is no precedent for this in his own experience or that of his family. He feels that he has somehow failed himself, his ancestors, his nation. But the nation, he says, has also failed him. He was close to tears, talking to me in a café in the main street of a river town. His angst was both practical and existential. And he pressed into my hands a copy of Peter Gell's paper – the fourth person to do so. He was choking up by now. He hammered the table and almost shouted: "Diatoms can't lie!"

*

South Australia is one of the best advertisements for the impact of the water returned to the environment at taxpayer expense. The Renmark Irrigation Trust has been using its infrastructure to deliver the water, and in January 2020 was awarded a platinum certification – the highest offered – by the international Alliance for Water Stewardship for its work in rehabilitating floodplains. Environmental watering sounds pretty, but it can be surprisingly crude. I was shown photos of a piece of PVC pipe sticking up out of the sand in a dry billabong bed. After the environmental watering, there was a full billabong. It was a reminder that even "environmental flows" must come through the plumbed landscape – that the natural is far out of reach.

Downstream from Renmark there is Banrock Station, a private vineyard and tourist centre near Kingston on the Murray. It was listed as a Ramsar wetland in 2002. During the millennium drought it was almost dead.

Now, largely thanks to the Commonwealth Environmental Water Holder, you can stand on the veranda of the winery, a glass in hand, and look over samphire floodplain and mallee, redgum forest and black box. You can watch the waterbirds and perhaps hear the endangered southern bell frog.

Further downstream, near Swan Reach, there is the Sugar Shack complex of streams and wetlands. It serves as a counter to the general picture of Indigenous involvement in the Plan – top-down consultation meetings which are then ignored or, as Badger Bates on the Lower Darling put it, "fake consultation." Sugar Shack is managed in partnership with the Ngarrindjeri.

So how are the environmental aims of the Basin Plan going – the rationale for the whole thing? It depends where you look. Bill Johnson is visibly distressed when he assesses his life's work, first as a park ranger with responsibility for the Macquarie Marshes, on the river between Narromine and Brewarrina, and then later as a water planner for the Basin Authority. There are some sites that are doing better, he says – wetlands managed carefully by locals working with environmental water. But overall, he says, the Murray–Darling system is near ecological collapse. He says:

> It's difficult to acknowledge this reality when one's working life has been based on another view – the hope and expectation that good sense, generosity and proper sharing of water will prevail. The system that we use to manage the rivers has failed. That's why people blame the drought. It means they don't need to examine the broader failing, and it deflects attention from that broader failing. A part of my anger and disappointment comes from the billions of dollars spent, the laws written, the plans and policies made, leaving the river system still collapsing because it has been undermined by bigger, more powerful interests, and their political influence.

Now, he thinks, "climate change will bring it all undone." Johnson has a particular attachment to the Macquarie Marshes. At the time of writing, they are on fire. He believes the rest will burn eventually. "I have already grieved it," he says.

Asked about this, Water Holder Jody Swirepik acknowledges the condition of the Marshes has suffered with the drought and now the fires. But things would be worse, she says, without environmental water. "We've spent years building the health and resilience of the Marshes using environmental water … The core area is in better condition and will have more capacity to bounce back than it would be if we hadn't done that." Johnson responds that this is at best a partial truth. "Drought has hit hard, but over-use of water for irrigation is the underlying cause, and that's been acknowledged for decades. Just saying it's the drought overlooks the underlying causes. The Marshes are only a fragment of what they were. Failing to acknowledge what we are losing means we will keep losing it." He goes on: "I do wonder: what have I achieved in thirty years of work on this stuff? I doubt if even one fish has lived one extra hour at Menindee because of my work."

Swirepik argues that it is a mistake to think the rivers of the Basin can be returned to how they were before dams and irrigation. Nobody wants that – the Basin supports national and community prosperity. But, she says, things are better than they would be without the Murray–Darling Basin Plan. She is optimistic. The drought has made everything challenging. There is still a long way to go in restoring the river system to health. She continues:

> But we have water allocated to the environment and we are already seeing the changes this can make. We have made a massive step change in Australia through substantial financial investment in the health of our rivers. I can't really see a circumstance where this commitment would be reversed.
>
> We are doing a remarkable thing to try and make the Basin sustainable and we don't celebrate this enough. The rest of the world looks to us to learn how the needs across industry sectors, the environment and critical human needs can be balanced. We have to keep working at this.

There are more dispassionate assessments that support the view some progress has been made. The Productivity Commission, in its five-year review published at the end of 2018, said there had been "substantial progress." About 20 per cent of the water available for consumption a decade ago had now been dedicated to the environment – 2000 gigalitres. But, said the commission, "the next phase is challenging." (The commission did not deal with the return flows issue.) The commission also gave a serve to the politicians. The challenges had been made harder because the process had "lacked transparency and candour ... Basin governments must make important changes now to ensure effective implementation. Failing to act will be costly for the environment and taxpayers, and undermine confidence that the Basin Plan has been worthwhile."

Since that report was issued, not much has changed, except that now New South Wales is barely in the Plan at all.

*

I interviewed the two bureaucrats most responsible for the implementation of the Murray–Darling Basin Plan, Jody Swirepik and Phillip Glyde, in Canberra in early December 2019. The city was wreathed in bushfire haze. It was the start of a horror summer in which the bush came to the cities in the form of smoke and dust.

In person, it is hard to associate Glyde with the allegations of maladministration and illegality laid at his door. He is mild-mannered, almost diffident. He admits to being told he is too longwinded. He is a career public servant who has served governments of both colours, as well as working for the OECD and the British government in agriculture and natural resource management. He has, surely, one of the hardest jobs in Australian bureaucracy – serving six governments, federal, territory and state.

Glyde can be frank, which sometimes exposes his own spin. In the weeks before our appointment, he had given Senate Estimates a frank assessment of what lay ahead for the summer. Communities had already run out of water. Conditions were "dire" in the north, and overall storages in the Southern Basin were at only 44 per cent. If there was no rain, southern irrigators faced more severe restrictions. There was little relief in sight. There would be more fish kills, more blue-green algae. Then he made two apparently contradictory assertions. He said that commitment to the Basin Plan was more important than ever because "when things are tough, available water is shared fairly between communities, irrigators and the river." But a few minutes before this, he had said: "In severe drought, when rivers cease to fully function, it's not always physically possible for governments to supply water, even for critical human needs. Water allocations and entitlements vary from state to state, and these differences mean that some entitlement holders have an allocation this season while others have little to none." How could those two statements both be true, I asked him.

I told him what I had seen – water scarce everywhere, the growers of St George still with some water while Wilcannia went dry. The irrigators of the Lower Darling tearing out their trees. Chris Brooks and the Southern Riverina Irrigators with zero allocations while their Victorian neighbours, on the other side of the river, had at least some.

He laid the blame on the state water-sharing agreements, "which has nothing to do with the Plan." New South Wales was suffering because it was in drought. Victoria was better off because it had had some rain. South Australia, with its guaranteed allowance, benefited most in the dry years and got least benefit from the wet. Added to that, Victoria allocated its water more conservatively than New South Wales, meaning there was more held back for a not-so-rainy day.

By "fair," then, he meant a pragmatic, qualified kind of fairness. "It's as fair as you can make it, given the fact that there's different geography and different history."

Over the course of two interviews, we traversed all the other criticisms of the Plan: the allegations that the science had been compromised in favour of a political fix. The huge uncertainties caused by floodplain harvesting and return flows. In response, he rarely dismissed a point made by one of his critics. Yes, he agreed, the Plan was devised on the basis of inadequate information. The models concerning the Northern Basin were particularly lacking. But that didn't mean that it was stupid to make a plan. That is the nature of natural resource management. Adjustments would have to be made, problems would have to be dealt with – but what was the option, other than to keep moving forward?

Pressed, he gave an eloquent analogy.

> There's a lot of things that happen in and around the Basin Plan that you could argue are not necessarily the most efficient and effective way to do it. But it's part of bringing everybody together. A petrol combustion engine is 33 per cent efficient. Two-thirds of the energy in the petrol is wasted, it doesn't drive you forward.
>
> People seem to expect that the Basin Plan will be absolutely 100 per cent efficient, squeaky ... But we have to recognise that we're starting with a really beat-up car that's almost dead, and that we're trying to upgrade it as we're driving it. Some of the expectations about perfection are completely and utterly unrealistic. That is not to say that it can all be politics. It can't be. It's got to be based in science. It's got to be based on good analysis. It's got to be the best you can do on the information you've got. Don't get me wrong. I'm not trying to say it's all political. I'm saying it's two things – a plan and a political compact.

Yet despite the political compromise, from the setting of the sustainable diversion limits up to Mick Keelty's weird new role, that compact isn't holding together very well. Which raises the question: could it have been done differently, given that all the compromises don't seem to have resulted in consensus or cohesion? For example, what would have happened if Labor and then the Coalition government had continued a determined program of water buybacks as the main way of recovering water? The total amount would probably have been recovered by now – and at much less cost to the taxpayer. Which would have freed up money that could have been better spent. More water buybacks might have hurt rural communities already under strain. But what if this was part of bold rural and regional policies of wisdom and sophistication, well thought-out and well communicated? What if the money saved was spent on health, education and schools in rural Australia?

Neither side of politics has such policies, nor shows any signs of developing them. The National Party is largely discredited, at least in the eyes of the farmers of the Southern Basin but also among many ordinary cotton growers. Rural Australia, no longer the heart of our national narrative, is too easily neglected. It has been governed piecemeal, and with cynicism, and the National Party has contributed to that. Some of the producer groups have made positive contributions, and some have been aggressive and short-sighted – on the wrong side of history. Developing visionary policies for rural Australia would take courageous leadership and enlightened politics. It is hard to find much evidence of either in the history of the Murray–Darling Basin. The exception, perhaps, is the fact that we have a Basin Plan at all.

And where is Labor? It's sad to see the party born in the shearing sheds of Queensland now so irrelevant in the politics of rural Australia. Stefano de Pieri, the well-known Mildura-based restaurateur, has recently involved himself in water politics and asks, "When is the city going to play a role? When will it get seriously interested? And by that I mean the Liberals have been happy to accommodate the National Party; and Labor, in its most recent self-scrutiny, has completely failed to say, 'Unless we develop proper regional, agricultural water policy, we will never get into power.' I say, 'Albanese, you are going nowhere without that!'"

There is a model for large-scale agricultural and environmental reform. Back in the 1980s, the issue was salinity. Groundwater was rising, bringing with it the ancient salts locked up in Australia's soils. The best science suggested it could wipe out most irrigated agriculture, and much dryland agriculture as well. Today, salinity is largely managed and under control. We won. Throughout the 1980s and '90s, there was an enormous community effort, led by local landholders, supported by state and federal government money. The story of that effort would take a book to tell. It included engineering works – deep plumbing of the landscape – in South Australia to intercept saline groundwater before it reached the river. It involved massive investment to better manage water and prevent it reaching the groundwater. In each agricultural area there were people – farmers – who stepped up. The changes were painful, but when they were introduced they were understood and accepted.

Could that have been done here? Everywhere I went in the Basin, farmers told me that the Murray–Darling Basin Plan was like an assault. It came from the top down. Local knowledge had been ignored or brushed aside. "They think we are just ignorant farmers." And, with the allegations of water theft and corruption, the willingness to sacrifice has been eroded. In every community I visited, there were people of intelligence and goodwill with the respect of their communities who could have been part of a locally led effort. I met people with relevant qualifications – environmental scientists and engineers – who were also part of the farming communities. Some of them made enemies of the water bureaucracy very early on, by questioning and criticising. They could have been treated as assets. Instead they were alienated and attacked. Some of them are still involved in water politics, but they have become weary, defensive and cynical. Too late, perhaps, the Authority and the Water Holder have tried to change tack, to take in local views.

Jeremy Morton, a rice grower near Moulamein, and a former president of the Ricegrowers Association, is more positive than many. He dates the change to top-down agricultural policy to the Hawke–Keating government and its economic rationalist reforms. Yes, it would have been hard to agree on a national Basin Plan at a local level, he says. There is lots of disagreement, but "if you get people into a room and present them with a problem, sooner or later they would have to hash something out, come up with a solution."

It might have been harder. It would almost certainly have been slower. It would have meant a program to build understanding across the Basin, of what was going on upstream and downstream. It would have meant addressing the underlying problem of the Murray–Darling Basin – that we no longer cohere, or know ourselves. We have a hole in our national identity and national narrative.

A different approach would have meant attempting to build a community out of the society of water users. And perhaps it wouldn't have worked. Glyde thinks it wouldn't have. The difference between salinity management and clawing water back for the environment, he says, is that the Basin Plan is asking people to give something up, rather than to save themselves from an immediate and a visible threat. He thinks it had to be macro policy, imposed from above. But he acknowledges that today the Authority continues to pay the price for top-down management. The Basin Plan is "a huge reform. The thing that was missing before the intervention of the Commonwealth was someone looking at this from a million-kilometre-square view, an elevated view of what's going on. And the criticism we often get is that we're making those judgments without enough of the local input – that we don't know enough about a particular valley. And I think that's a fair criticism." Glyde is trying to decentralise, opening up regional offices and employing locals. In the meantime, "We have an average of more than one meeting a day in the Basin. But it's never going to be enough."

He's right. And the lack of community support and trust means that one possible future for the Plan is that it will collapse under the weight of resentment and litigation. The Barkandji are certainly considering a case. The possibility of a High Court challenge, perhaps by the states litigating against each other, hangs like a shadow over the future.

*

In late January 2020, David Littleproud gave the clearest sign of his tenure that he was committed to keeping the Plan alive. He informed the NSW water minister, Melinda Pavey, that because the state's water resource plans had not been submitted by the already extended deadline, he would withhold millions of dollars in federal funding. In theory the Murray–Darling

Basin Authority is now empowered to ride over the top of New South Wales and determine the management of water itself, including enforcing the recovery of the NSW share of 450 gigalitres. In practice, the politics make that next to impossible. Littleproud left New South Wales with an out. If it submitted some of the least sensitive plans as soon as possible, it would give him "some confidence in respect to New South Wales's ongoing commitment to Basin Plan implementation." It looks like a game of chicken. One side or the other has to flinch. At the time of writing, the new federal water minister, Keith Pitt, has yet to signal his attitude.

New South Wales – the state that contains the largest share of the Basin – has dropped the ball on compliance, possibly harboured criminality and corruption, dragged the chain on Plan implementation and now threatens to leave altogether. What does "Can the Plan" actually mean? There is no other method on the table for pegging back a resource everyone agrees has been over-allocated. If there is a strategy at work in New South Wales, other than raw, unprincipled politics, it is hard to discern.

Meanwhile, Glyde's approach – remaking the car as you drive it – creates a political problem. It means that, despite the reform weariness everywhere in the Basin, the process is far from over. It may never be over.

One of the strongest criticisms of the Basin Plan is that the sustainable diversion limits were calculated on the basis of historical flows only – with no account of climate change. Professor Ross Garnaut, who conducted the 2008 climate change review for the incoming Rudd government, has commented: "The Murray–Darling Basin Plan … was built, at best, on hope. At worst, on obfuscation." The Garnaut Review predicted that, on current trends, the Murray–Darling Basin would lose around half its irrigated agricultural output by mid-century and about 92 per cent by 2100, due to drought, decreased rainfall and runoff. You won't find politically unpalatable figures like that anywhere in the documents surrounding the Murray–Darling Basin Plan.

I met only one climate change denier in the Basin. This man thought the whole thing was a lie, a plot by the United Nations to keep people scared and compliant. But in most cases when I raised the issue with farmers, the response was a million-mile stare. If Garnaut's prediction is right, then all this work, all the meetings, all the politics – none of it would be enough. The most optimistic response was from Scott Armstrong, the cotton grower in St George: "We will adapt." We have to hope that he is right. We have to hope that governments might be up to the task of speaking frankly to him, and helping him and his children to make those adaptations.

Professor Mike Young remembers that when he was advising the government on the Plan he argued for a different way of setting the caps on use. Rather than locking in a fixed amount of water to be consumed in the future – the sustainable diversion limit – he suggested that a base flow – not to be touched, and used to run the river – be decided. The water for consumption and for the environment should then be set as shares of the remainder – not as a fixed amount. There would be no buying back of water, just an agreement on shares. The advantage of this system, he argues, would be that the allocations to the shares could be pegged to "dynamic indicators" that reflected the changing nature of the system – perhaps flows at the Murray Mouth or local rainfall. Thus, the system would automatically adjust to change, including climate change. Young recalls a very difficult discussion with then water minister Malcolm Turnbull. "I was closely involved in the drafting, and I was arguing very hard, and Malcolm said to me, 'Mike, it is time to put this to bed. It is better to go with what we have. You are no longer being useful.' Now I think that this was probably the right call. It was a political call, taking into account the difficulty and the tensions between states and federal government negotiations. Turnbull said, 'We've got an opportunity to get this legislation through now. I need you to support it publicly and stop trying to improve it.'"

I asked Glyde about Young's proposal. It would have been possible, he says, if the states had agreed to refer the necessary powers to the Commonwealth. In the absence of that, the fixed SDLs were required both for legal reasons and also for "bringing people along reasons." He adds that perhaps in twenty or thirty years, "in Basin Plan Mark Four or Five," something like Young's scheme could be introduced. "The states would have to agree, of course. Hopefully we might get there, but it's just not politically feasible to do that now."

And I was imagining what the farmers I had met would say if they heard Glyde talking about more Basin Plans, in decades to come.

Along with his proposal to ban the export of cotton, Senator Rex Patrick has made a more substantial, if heroically ambitious, contribution: a bill to provide for a referendum to amend the Australian constitution and correct what he sees as the error of the founding fathers in giving power over water to the states. Patrick has a game plan. He has negotiated the setting up of a parliamentary committee looking at the multi-jurisdictional issues of Basin management – yet another of the numerous inquiries into Basin matters. He predicted to me in early October 2019 that it would be another "dreadful" summer. The collapse of the system would become self-evident. The committee would report towards the end of 2020, and he expected it to nail the problems. Then, he said, he was prepared to push hard, and use the balance of power, to get the referendum. But if the states can't achieve consensus over the implementation of the Basin Plan, it is hard to believe that such a referendum, requiring a majority of votes in a majority of states, could ever succeed.

*

As I was finishing this essay, it rained over much of the Basin. Scott Armstrong, in St George, told me there was suddenly "lots of water around … so relieved." It was predicted that river flows in the Barwon–Darling might reach Tilpa, and perhaps even as far as Wilcannia. Rachel Strachan and Alan Whyte in the Lower Darling were part of a campaign for the flow to be embargoed. "We are pushing for 'freshwater to Wentworth' to be a higher priority than any irrigation anywhere," Whyte told me. But the next day the NSW government announced a three-day lift on an embargo on floodplain harvesting in the Border Rivers region, allowing cotton growers to harvest the flow. Strachan commented: "That is the cream of the flood." Graeme McCrabb, the Menindee farmer propelled to national prominence by the fish kill, was once again contacting journalists. He told *The Guardian* he was "heartbroken ... you should see it: mussels dying on the side of the river, dead fish every day. Words just don't describe how terrible it is here." New South Wales had used satellite surveillance of Queensland to see if the flow was being intercepted by floodplain harvesting, before effectively allowing their own growers to do the same.

A few days later, Ian Cole – the man who negotiated those fateful late changes to the Barwon–Darling water resource plan – was keen to avoid any suggestion that he was to blame this time around. He told *The Sydney Morning Herald* he had been at a restaurant with irrigators and NSW water minister Melinda Pavey in the days before the rain. They had discussed how the expected flow would be managed. "She said, 'How would you like to handle it?'" Cole claimed. He said he had argued for the first flush of the flow to be left untouched and allowed to go down the river without any extraction for irrigation. Pavey, meanwhile, said the decision to allow three days of floodplain harvesting had been made by her department. The Victorian water minister, Lisa Neville, attacked both the Queensland and NSW governments and wrote to the new federal minister, Keith Pitt, asking that Mick Keelty investigate the harvesting of the flow by both states.

Rain after such a punishing drought was a wonderful thing, but if anybody had expected it to make water politics easier, they would have been wrong. It seems Keelty, still apparently without real power, may have yet another job to do.

So many compromises, so many reviews, so many political fixes over so many years – all to keep the battered jalopy of the Murray–Darling Basin Plan on the road. Yet still the political compact threatens to break.

As I finish this essay, the flow from the blessed rain is approaching Bourke.

*

It is strange which memories stay with you after a long road trip – so many hours of distant horizons and dust. The image that keeps returning to me is that small gesture between the drivers on the remote roads back of Bourke – the lift of the finger from the steering wheel, with its implicit message of shared endeavour.

The political obstacles, the hate, the unfairness and the potentially catastrophic gaps in our knowledge obscure what an achievement it would be for the Murray–Darling Basin Plan to succeed. A voluntary scheme to peg back use of an overstretched resource would be close to unprecedented in the world. Perhaps, in the face of the evidence, it might mean there is hope for our system of government, for our politics, and for us all.

Standing on the highest point of Hindmarsh Island in Lake Alexandrina, you can get a view of the great sheet of lake, of seaspray rising from the ocean, of paddocks and the toytown of Goolwa on the mainland and the Adelaide Hills in the distance.

And from the southern beaches you can see the mouth of the Murray – a break in the sand-dune isthmuses that divide lake from ocean, and the dredges – red-green industrial machinery against the dunes – pumping out the sand so the river can dawdle its way to the sea. Viewed from above, or on Google Earth, the Murray Mouth is a blue-green channel running through sandhills that look like flesh.

Hindmarsh Island is suspended above the narrow channel like a baby waiting to be born. This is the root of the tree, where it all begins. Or where it ends.

SOURCES

Interim Inspector-General of Murray–Darling Basin Water Resources Mick Keelty declined a request for an interview to inform this essay. NSW Minister for Water, Property and Housing Melinda Pavey was approached, but her office did not respond to requests in time. Ian Cole did not return phone calls and emails seeking an interview.

1 "recent reimaginings": Leah Purcell, *The Drover's Wife*, Penguin, Melbourne, 2019.

3 "about 86,000 farms": Australian Bureau of Statistics, *7121.0 Agricultural Commodities, Australia, 2015–16*, ABS, Canberra, 30 April 2019.

6 "a post-truth world": R. Quentin Grafton, Matt Colloff, Virginia Marshall and John Williams, "Confronting a 'post-truth water world' in the Murray–Darling Basin, Australia", *Water Alternatives*, no. 13, 2019, pp. 1–28.

6 "The remaining 4 per cent": Land and Water Australia, *National Land and Water Resources Audit*, 2000, Table 3, p. 25.

6 "About 500 gigalitres": Murray–Darling Basin Commission, *Murray–Darling Basin Water Resources Fact Sheet*, MDBC, July 2006.

7 "In fact, the releases": Peter Hannam, "Water Minister Melinda Pavey ignored the state's own water releases", *The Sydney Morning Herald*, 3 November 2019.

11 "the word 'rival'": Philip Pregill and Nancy Volkman, *Landscapes in History: Design and Planning in the Eastern and Western Traditions*, Wiley and Sons, New York, 1999.

12 "That time may be coming": Nicholas Kelly, "A bridge? The troubled history of inter-state water resources and constitutional limitations on state use of water", *UNSW Law Journal*, vol. 30, no. 3, 2007.

14 "He remarked": John Howard, Press conference, Perth, 24 July 2007.

16 "Wong says today": Margaret Simons, *Penny Wong: Passion and Principle*, Black Inc., Melbourne, 2019.

16 "journalists wrote it up as a bribe": Greg Kelton and Kim Wheatley, "Dear SA: You were right but it took an extra billion dollars", *Adelaide Advertiser*, 27 March 2008.

17 "legislated drought": Quoted in Bret Walker, *Murray–Darling Basin Royal Commission, Report*, 29 January 2019, p. 172.

17 "the Windsor report": House of Representatives, Standing Committee on Regional Australia, *Of Drought and Flooding Rains: Inquiry into the Impact of the Guide to the Murray–Darling Basin Plan. Report*, Commonwealth of Australia, Canberra, May 2011.

18 "there is scope": Murray–Darling Basin Authority, *Response to the South Australian Royal Commission*, MDBA, February 2019.

18 "time to move on": Walker, p. 172.

19 "everyone understood": Walker, p. 216.

20 "[manipulating] science": ibid.

20 "a story of cynical disregard": Walker, p. 11.

23 "an international conspiracy": Australian Citizens' Party, "Murray–Darling Basin Plan Was Always a Fraud", Media release, 11 July 2019.

23 "Eddie McGuire": "Eddie McGuire: Water baron?" *The Hot Breakfast*, Triple M, 19 July 2019.

27 "there is evidence": NSW Natural Resources Commission, *Final Report: Review of the Water Sharing Plan for the Barwon Darling Unregulated and Alluvial Water Sources 2012*, September 2019.

31 "The provisions benefit": ibid.

32 "the river was already": Jacqueline Breen and Gavin Coote, "Largest native title claim in NSW acknowledges Barkandji people in state's far west", *ABC News* (online), 16 June 2015.

34 "a dispiriting instance" etc: Walker, p. 316.

34 "Joyce wrote a letter", "in which he backtracked", and "The South Australian Minister": Walker, p. 409.

35 "to fuck off": Natalie Kotsios and Tory Shepherd, "SA Water Minister Ian Hunter in foul mouthed tirade at fellow politicians", *Adelaide Now*, 18 November 2016.

37 "It had nothing to do": Paige Cockburn, "Menindee mass fish death fury escalates, NSW Police and Minister at odds", *ABC News* (online), 15 January 2019.

39 "Barilaro was issuing": Peter Hannam and Alexandra Smith, "Barilaro's backing of federal Murray–Darling Basin royal commission muddies the waters", *The Sydney Morning Herald*, 31 January 2019.

39 "serious deficiencies": Australian Academy of Science, *Investigation of the Causes of Mass Fish Kills in the Menindee Region NSW over the Summer of 2018–2019*, 18 February 2019.

45 "sop to the Green movement": ABC News, "Toorale deal won't help lower lakes: Wong", 11 September 2008; ABC News, "Opposition brands Toorale sale 'anti-rural'", 11 September 2008.

45 "Wong announced": Mike Foley, "Toorale in flood but Darling dry despite Wong's $24 million water deal", *Farm Online National*, 29 May 2019.

51 "claimed he had been told": Anne Davies, "NSW cotton grower faces more charges over water pumped from Barwon river", *The Guardian*, 21 May 2019.

52 "Self-interested parties": Brewarrina Shire Council, Submission to the South Australian Murray–Darling Basin Royal Commission.

53 "increasing pressure", "insufficiently urgent": Ken Matthews, *Independent Investigation into NSW Water Management and Compliance: Advice on implementation*, NSW Government, 24 November 2017.

55 "Australian Floodplain Association President": Daniel Pedersen, "Taking water from the top means less at the bottom, say irrigators", *The Land*, 27 March 2019.

59 "Our nation's food bowl": Maryanne Slattery and Roderick Campbell, *Briefing Note: First steps to fix the Murray-Darling Basin*, The Australia Institute, 10 May 2019.

63 "We, the Committee": Gavin Atkins, "Let the Tank Stream run free", Border Rivers Food and Fibre website, 16 December 2010.

72 "She became": Shortly before this essay was completed, Slattery left the Australia Institute to start a consultancy, Slattery and Johnson, with another former Authority employee, Bill Johnson.

72 "He has been described": Ean Higgins, "Irrigator Chris Brooks taps into a torrent of anger on water 'theft'", *The Australian*, 30 December 2019.

78 "overbank transfers": Murray–Darling Basin Authority, Statement to *60 Minutes* on River Murray Operations, 28 October 2019.

81 "They were not entirely successful": Slattery, Campbell and Quicke.

81 "two of them received": Maryanne Slattery, Roderick Campbell and Audrey Quicke, *Dam Shame – The Hidden Dams in Australia*, Report, Australia Institute, October 2019.

81 "twice as expensive": Productivity Commission, p. 107.

84 "Grafton admits": John Williams and Quentin Grafton, "Missing in action: possible effects of water recovery on stream and river flows in the Murray–Darling Basin, Australia", *Australasian Journal of Water Resources*, vol. 23, 2019.

85 "Desperate men": Warwick Long, "Dumped gravel and rock blocks environmental water from flowing into Murray–Darling forest", ABC Victoria, *Country Hour*, 23 September 2019.

85 "We're trying": Warwick Long, "Effigy of federal water minister David Littleproud floats towards SA in Murray–Darling Basin Plan protest", ABC Victoria, *Country Hour*, 20 September 2019.

87 "huge win": Kath Sullivan and Clint Jasper, "'Can the Plan' protesters say they've brokered a deal with federal water minister and Mick Keelty", *ABC Rural* (online), 3 December 2019.

87 "to find buckets": Sophie Boyd, "Ministerial council to meet over Murray Darling Basin Plan", *Port Macquarie News* (online), 7 December 2019.

87 "We have turned": Southern Riverina Irrigators, "Brighter future after inquiry meetings", Southern Riverina Irrigators website, 29 January 2020.

87 "lauded Littleproud's leadership": Mick Keelty with Fran Kelly, *RN Breakfast*, 5 December 2019.

87–8 "Some State Ministers": Murray Darling Ministerial Council, Communiqué, 20 December 2019.

88 "The financial and mental stress": Kath Sullivan, "Inside the room as the Murray–Darling's top cop Mick Keelty meets irrigators", *ABC Rural* (online), 25 January 2020.

88 "Littleproud denies it": Kath Sullivan and Clint Jasper, "Murray–Darling investigation under pressure, as Littleproud says no extra water for farmers", *ABC Rural* (online), 4 December 2019.

88 "not ideal": Lucy Barbour, "David Littleproud returns to agriculture as Nationals change jobs in Scott Morrison's new-look frontbench", *ABC News* (online), 9 February 2020.

89 "further stall": James Bennett, "A return to Canberra for farmers?", *Deniliquin Pastoral Times*, 18 February 2020.

90 "He had acquired": Samantha Townsend, "Update: An effigy water minister David Littleproud is travelling around 12km a day down the Murray", *The Land*, 20 September 2019; Warwick Long, "Effigy of federal water minister David Littleproud floats towards SA in Murray–Darling Basin Plan protest", ABC Victoria, *Country Hour*, 20 September 2019.

90 "he was fished out": Geoff Adams, "Effigy floats", *Country News*, 29 October 2019.

90 "particularly successful": Victorian Environmental Water Holder, "Swamp wallabies return to forest", VEHW website, 12 December 2019.

92 "He probably didn't want to do it": Hugh Schuitemaker, "'No SA benefit' from Keelty's MDB inquiry", *Murray Pioneer*, 29 January 2020, p. 3.

93 "evaporation in South Australia accounts": Vincent Kotwicki, "The nature of evaporation from Lake Alexandrina", *Water Down Under 94: Surface Hydrology and Water Resources Papers*, Preprints of Papers, Barton, ACT: Institution of Engineers, Australia, 1994, pp. 385–90.

94 "vigorously investigate": Suzanna Sheed, Media release, 11 September 2019.

94 "resulting co-authored paper": Jennie Fluin, Peter Gell, Deborah Hayes, John Tibby and Gary Hancock, "Paleolimnological evidence for the independent evolution of neighbouring terminal lakes, the Murray–Darling Basin, Australia", October 2007, vol. 591, issue 1, pp. 117–34.

95 "the science of the lower lakes": Murray–Darling Basin Authority, *The Lower Lakes Independent Science Review*, MDBA, 15 January 2020.

99 "lacked transparency": Productivity Commission.

100 "when things are tough": Senate Rural and Regional Affairs and Transport Legislation Committee, Estimates, *Hansard*, 25 October 2019.

105 "some confidence": Kylar Loussikian, "Federal takeover looms as NSW fails to complete river plans", *The Sydney Morning Herald*, 26 January 2020.

105 "The Murray–Darling Basin Plan": Ross Garnaut, *Superpower: Australia's Low-Carbon Opportunity*, Black Inc., Melbourne, 2019, p. 5.

108 "heartbroken": Anne Davies, " NSW green light to irrigators to harvest rainfall angers downstream residents", *The Guardian*, 12 February 2020.

108 "New South Wales had used" and "The Victorian water minister": "States at war over Murray–Darling water grab", *The Australian*, 20 February 2020.

108 "'How would you like to handle it?'": Harriet Alexander, "'How would you like to handle it?': The minister, the irrigators and a flood", *The Sydney-Morning Herald*, 20 February 2020.

Amy King

Peter Hartcher's essay homes in on what he sees as the "essential starting point" for Australia in its relations with China: the question "What does China want from Australia?" This is an interesting question, but not the right one. By framing it in this way, Hartcher places Australia in the passive position of waiting to see what China wants and then responding as best it can.

This critique is not just a semantic one. Hartcher argues that what China wants is "as much power and influence over Australia as it can possibly get, using fair means or foul." But what China wants is only half the story. Influence is a two-way street, as research by my colleague Evelyn Goh at the Australian National University reminds us. China's ability to influence other countries depends as much on the choices, decision-making processes and domestic institutions of these countries, as well as the international arrangements that they make, as it does on China's power, pressure or skill. It is no different in Australia. What is most remarkable about Hartcher's engaging accounts of Chinese attempts to influence Australian politicians and journalists is his demonstration that these efforts have consistently failed. Not only did Joe Hockey, Stephen Conroy, Bill Shorten, Penny Wong, Richard Marles and John Garnaut resist Chinese attempts to persuade or coerce, by Hartcher's account they also hardened their views towards China as a result. Indeed, the only "successful" case of Chinese Communist Party influence over an Australian politician was arguably that of Sam Dastyari, whose willingness to parrot China's position on the South China Sea brought a rapid end to his parliamentary career.

Hartcher acknowledges the consistent failure of Chinese attempts to "intrude" in Australian political and economic life. But he appears unconvinced by his own argument that there are limits to Beijing's influence, or that Australia has the capacity to shape the nature of its relationship with China. Instead, he portrays Australia as fundamentally vulnerable to China's overtures. He quotes at length former ASIO chief Duncan Lewis, who claims Australia faces an "existential threat" as a result of China's "unprecedented" foreign interference activities. Having started from the passive position of asking "What does China want from Australia?" Hartcher can't help but dismiss his own evidence and conclude that our politicians, journalists, businesses, universities and citizens are vulnerable to China and in need of protection by an increasingly powerful ASIO. By this flawed argument, he concludes, disturbingly, that we must give our intelligence agencies the right to vet those who run for parliament in this country.

Hartcher also dramatically underestimates the extent to which China's own character and behaviour have often worked to limit its influence, both in Australia and around the world. Chinese economic statecraft in South Korea and elsewhere has undermined the country's reputation as a reliable, market-based economic partner, while Xi Jinping's creeping authoritarianism and human rights abuses at home have raised doubts about the desirability of a more Chinese-centred international order. Hartcher echoes perennial fears in Canberra that Asia-Pacific countries are being "bought off" by China's lucrative foreign aid and infrastructure spending. There's little evidence of this. A major study by AidData found that Chinese spending of US$120 billion in infrastructure and other financial diplomacy in South and Central Asia since 2000 has not translated into countries siding with China on contentious issues, or automatically winning over public support. Where China has been successful in gaining support on the world stage, it has commonly been because its policies or values align with those of other countries, particularly in the developing world: providing investment in much-needed physical infrastructure, giving them greater representation in global institutions, and preserving an international order that respects plural values and diverse systems of government.

At home in Australia, China's so-called "influence operations" have not only failed, they've had precisely the opposite of their intended effect. China's efforts to cultivate influence – through both overt and covert means – have resulted in a notable hardening of Australian attitudes in recent years. As Hartcher notes, the authoritative Lowy Institute poll of Australian attitudes about international affairs saw a 20 per cent decline in Australian levels of trust of China between 2018 and 2019. Yet again Hartcher is strangely unconvinced by his own evidence. Despite noting that Australians possess a "realistic" scepticism in their appraisals of China, his essay leans heavily on unsubstantiated assertions that Australian society is especially vulnerable to Chinese "infiltration," or that China has already "bought control" of Australia's economy and political system. As a result, Hartcher interprets cases like the United Front's attempts to put on concerts in the Sydney and Melbourne town halls celebrating Mao Zedong as an example of how Australian naivety is being exploited by CCP interest groups. But an alternative reading is that these concert bookings generated vigorous debate and criticism about Mao's leadership within the Australian Chinese community – precisely what one would hope for and expect in a healthy democratic society.

Hartcher rightly points to paralysis in Australian strategy on China. But the starting point for developing this strategy cannot be a defensive reaction to what China wants from Australia. Instead, it must be a forward-looking answer to the question "What does Australia want from China?" and, more importantly, "What can Australia achieve on the global stage?" Answering these questions will require rigorous evidence-based debate about China and the reasons why it remains so vitally important to Australia.

Rather than weakening our democratic institutions, or requiring a slavishly bipartisan line on China, as Hartcher suggests, we should remind ourselves that robust debate and critique of government policy is not a sign of disloyalty or of being pro-Beijing, but instead represents the contestability that is at the heart of an effective democratic system.

Amy King

RED
FLAG

Correspondence

David Walker

I began reading Peter Hartcher's essay in China. I was teaching an MA class at Beijing Foreign Studies University on Australian responses to the rise of Asia from the mid-nineteenth century to the present. I had taught variations on this theme during my time as BHP Chair of Australian Studies at Peking University from 2013 to 2016. In the three months I was in Beijing late last year the skies were clear and the air quality good. Meanwhile, Australia was on fire. I left China more convinced than ever that the biggest national security threat facing our continent and our immediate region is not China, but climate change.

Hartcher's essay is not confined to the here and now. He speculates on where China will be in 2049, when the Chinese Communist Party will have been in power for a century. But will it make it that far? Following the seventy-year anniversary of the CCP last year there has been discussion of the lifespan of authoritarian regimes. As I read this literature, it seems that reaching a century would defy precedent and is far from assured. In this same timeframe, the world will be dealing with the accelerating impacts of climate change. In our region these impacts may well be catastrophic for Pacific nations, generating large flows of climate refugees. And should we think of the residents and visitors in Mallacoota at the turn of the decade as climate refugees?

The next thirty years promise to be turbulent and difficult to predict. Hartcher should be applauded for offering a roadmap to this future. He is emboldened to do so, it seems to me, because he appears to know where China wants to be in 2049 and implies that what China wants China will get. We are told that where China wants to be in 2049 is clearly spelt out in the secret and sinister "Document 9." Hartcher tells us that this document outlines CCP plans to achieve a tighter, more authoritarian grip on power within China while also working to make China the dominant global power. What credence should be given to Document 9 is an open question. More important is the willingness to believe that a document written in 2012 can be flawlessly implemented to accomplish stated goals by 2049.

This mode of thinking takes us into Orientalist territory, bringing to the surface yet again deeply held and persistent fears. For well over a century Australia has produced a body of speculative writing and conspiratorial thinking about a threatening Asia. The late-nineteenth and early-twentieth century produced invasion stories in which the challenge arose not from China's remarkable/disturbing cohesion but from its collapse. As the Qing dynasty fell apart, pundits worried that "floods" of Chinese would flow into "empty" Australia, wiping out European settlement. Populous China, a country in turbulent disarray, torn by rebellion within and by the encroachment of hostile foreign powers, was seen as a distinct threat to Australia's survival. This perceived threat prompted massive increases in defence spending in the early years of the new Commonwealth, from 1901 to 1914. In this way, imagined vulnerabilities had very real political and budgetary consequences.

China, at that point in our history, appeared to present two problems: there were far too many Chinese and they seemed able to act collectively in ways Europeans could not. One chapter in my book *Anxious Nation* is titled "One Hundred Act as One" – a phrase taken from goldrush Australia. On the goldfields the Chinese seemed to work together in uncanny ways, like bees or ants in their hives or anthills. A similar unease surfaced at the opening ceremony of the Beijing Olympics, when thousands of perfectly coordinated Chinese marched, danced and waved placards. Were these real human beings or automata?

If the collapse of China under the Qing posed a grave threat, so too did China united under communism from 1949. Visiting Australia in the late 1950s, the British writer and broadcaster Malcolm Muggeridge warned Australians that with Mao fully in control it would only be a matter of fifteen to twenty years before Australia was overrun. Journalist and author Donald Horne picked up on the widespread fatalism of this time, which was summed up, he believed, in the oft-heard phrase "we don't have a chance."

The Catholic intellectual B.A. Santamaria was very clear about what was going to happen to Australia. In the late 1950s, he was at his most influential as a Cold War warrior, broadcaster and newspaper columnist. Where his friend Muggeridge had wandered around sniffing the breeze in his endearing way, Santamaria had laid his hands on actual documents, hard evidence that revealed China's plans. It would all happen in the next twenty years. China would take control of Australia. China's planned "political warfare" or "revolution by stealth" would unfold in three carefully calculated stages, culminating in the complete incorporation of Australia into the Chinese "co-prosperity sphere." Japan's co-prosperity plan for Asia had been recycled to the Chinese. In formulating his views, Santamaria was influenced by Lenin's prophecy of 1918 that for communists the road to Paris and world domination lay through Beijing. There it was. Lenin had a plan and it was being implemented. The fall of Australia, while not central, was certainly part of that long-term strategy.

Santamaria was not the only figure to have acquired written proof of Chinese intentions. Even the *Murrumbidgee Irrigator* had documents proving that Mao was planning the "ultimate absorption of Australia into the Communist empire of the East." The front cover of Denis Warner's *Hurricane from China* (1961) read, "What you MUST know about Mao Tse-Tung's plan for world conquest." In 1961, the invincible Mao had plunged China into the calamitous Great Leap Forward, at a cost of up to 30 million lives and perhaps the worst famine in Chinese history.

Of course, it does not follow that because warnings about a threatening Asia/China proved wrong in the past that today's new warnings must also be wrong. But any application of "due diligence" principles would suggest that we should look very closely at the history of Australian predictions about the rise of Asia/China. This is not something we are keen to do. What do these recurrent anxieties about losing our nation to Asia tell us? What is the expertise or knowledge of the people issuing these warnings? What evidence do they bring to bear and how reliable is it? What kind of impact are they aiming for? Finally, any case that is made for a negative or apocalyptic scenario involving a threatening Asia/China should be "stress-tested" by measuring the case in favour against the opposing case. It is not naive to do this. It is simply prudent.

While in Beijing recently I asked a senior Chinese academic at Peking University, someone with considerable Australian experience, what was going on in Hong Kong. I put it to them that surely the Chinese leadership would be getting very sophisticated briefings about the situation. Beijing would know a great deal more than it was prepared to reveal. My colleague was wholly unconvinced, arguing that the Chinese government probably had very little real understanding of what motivated the demonstrators in Hong Kong and little idea of how to resolve the conflict. This person added that if Beijing knew so little about Hong Kong, it seemed likely they would know even less about other, more distant societies. This view appears to be borne out by Hong Kong's recent municipal elections. It came as a great surprise to Beijing that its candidates were trounced. Where is the evidence of a masterful plan and how is it going? To that we can now add pushback from Indonesia and a negative response to Beijing in the recent Taiwanese general election.

Around this time, I attended a two-day forum in Beijing on developments in what the Chinese call "Oceania" – what we think of as the Pacific Islands. After several New Zealand academics had delivered nuanced accounts of Pacific Island cultures and political systems and their shared concern about climate change, I sensed that one of my Chinese colleagues was becoming quite impatient. At question time, he announced his Pacific solution. These small, doomed nations, he argued, just had to be summarily picked up and planted somewhere else. There was a problem and here was the obvious, if culturally insensitive solution from a senior Chinese exponent of international relations.

A society that has made brilliant economic and technical achievements over the last forty years may at the same time be culturally insular and poorly equipped to acknowledge that different ways of seeing the world might have their own merit. China can often appear (and be) harsh, clumsy and bullying when it meets societies, cultures and opinions its government does not endorse. I have no reason to doubt Hartcher's account of the harassment, bullying and attempted bribery meted out to Australian journalist John Garnaut. Why would he make it up?

However, in the period when I was a visiting academic in China (even as a professor in its top university), I saw no red envelopes stuffed with cash, received no tempting inducements to change my opinions and there was no attempt to influence what I taught. That said, I do know of one visiting Australian academic who was not invited back after a student complained that he had shown a video critical of China to his class. Chinese academics will protest that they are free to discuss all manner of issues, but I remain unconvinced.

When it comes to the "China threat," where does the Australian public stand? Drawing on Lowy Institute polling, Hartcher demonstrates that, while growing more uneasy, the public remains fairly measured in its response to China's rise. When compared with citizens of other nations, Australians are neither extremely fearful nor unconcerned. But where the public sits does not correspond that well with what our security services are saying. Hartcher draws heavily on the opinions of former director of ASIO Duncan Lewis. None of his opinions is questioned, including his claim that China poses an "existential threat" to Australia. To be clear, Lewis claims that China is not simply seeking to interfere in Australian affairs in wholly unacceptable ways, but has a plan to subvert and control the nation. For him, Australia is the test case, the "canary in the mine" for China's global ambition. For ASIO, the Australian public is not worried enough when it comes to China. The Coalition appears to agree: its task is to have the public worry more about China and less about climate change.

The problem for the public, myself included, is that ASIO works in an extremely shadowy world. We are instructed to heed its warnings and trust its judgment while being kept in the dark about the extent, depth and effectiveness of foreign influence from all quarters. We have seen the absurd spectacle of Senator Jacqui Lambie handing her vote to the government after a "national security" briefing. The government denies there was a deal, and our democratically elected senator will not reveal anything about the briefing. Some years after the spectacle of "on-water matters," the government runs the real risk of turning national security into a selectively applied and all too convenient expedient to be turned on and off as opinion polls dictate. Will the latest dip in the polls mean a renewed focus on national security and the China threat?

Hartcher recommends a federal Independent Commission Against Corruption and effectively implemented regulations around foreign political donations. These seem sensible measures. We also need well-informed, disciplined debate and, as Hartcher argues, much more confidence in the strength and appeal of our own society and its democratic institutions. Our democratic freedoms are an important reason why so many Chinese want to settle here.

David Walker

Correspondence

John West

Peter Hartcher's recent Quarterly Essay provides an excellent, informative and insightful analysis of the challenges Australia faces in managing its deepening relationship with China. But like many important works of analysis, it raises just as many questions as it answers, a few of which I will address here.

The first point is that Hartcher may be guilty of overestimating China's historical economic and political power. He highlights the economic power of China when he notes that "China's economy was the biggest in the world for at least half a millennium, until as recently as 1820." While that may be true, over this same period China progressively slipped behind Western Europe and especially the United Kingdom in terms of GDP per capita, which is a better indicator of economic and technological sophistication than total economy size. Although Chinese and Western European GDP per capita were similar for the first millennium of the Common Era, by the year 1500 Western Europe's GDP per capita had leapt 30 per cent ahead of China's. And by 1820, Western Europe's GDP per capita was more than double that of China, and by 1950 it was more than ten times China's. The reality is that for much of the past 500 years (in fact, until the reforms launched by Deng Xiaoping in 1978) China had a stagnant and relatively declining economy. In other words, its economy was big thanks to its enormous population, but backward. And this economic stagnation made it highly vulnerable to outside forces like the Manchus, who conquered China in the seventeenth century and created the Qing dynasty, and also Japan and several Western countries, which invaded China in the nineteenth and twentieth centuries. Overestimating China's historical power is now a widespread trend, and gives the impression that China's renaissance is returning the country to its natural dominant position in global affairs. The reality is that for more than 500 years, China was a fading power with a relatively declining and stagnant economy.

Second, Hartcher mentions some of the challenges facing the Chinese economy today. Indeed, despite its rapid development in these past few decades, China still has a big but backward economy, with a GDP per capita that is only one-quarter that of the United States. And China faces significant challenges, such as its enormous debt, rapidly ageing population, weak productivity, and trade and geopolitical tensions with the United States and other Western countries. Chinese productivity is only 30 per cent of that of world leaders like the US and Germany.

In this context, one issue not explored by Hartcher is how Australia's relationship with China might be affected if China fell into a scenario of long-term economic stagnation (as Japan, Asia's previous superstar, has done) or if it succumbed to an economic crisis like some Asian countries did two decades ago. The Australian economy would suffer from such a scenario, given our close economic relations. But the Chinese Communist Party, which relies on strong economic growth as a source of political legitimacy, would likely ramp up nationalism to maintain popular support. Such nationalism could take many forms, such as assertive behaviour towards Australia's close friends, like Japan. It could also involve more coercive behaviour towards Australia's ethnic Chinese population. Further, a weakening economy could see more Chinese citizens seeking to leave China for countries like Australia, as well as even more capital flight.

In short, a China that gets bogged in economic stagnation and becomes more paranoid and insecure may well prove an even more dangerous country to deal with. We see this today with Russia, which is an economic basket case, but is flailing about on the international stage, causing havoc wherever it goes.

Lastly, Hartcher lavishes praise on the Chinese state: "Imperial China, a world leader in technology, also pioneered the capable, modern nation-state. It took Europe almost two millennia to catch up. China is again thrusting to the forefront of technological know-how and pioneering a more effective nation-state." While this is true, it is also true that China has never had the rule of law, by which the country's highest political authority should also obey the law. Even today, the Chinese Communist Party is a law unto itself, and China's judiciary is highly politicised and corrupt. "Constitutionalism" is a taboo subject in China. Nor have China's rulers ever been subject to "downward accountability" to the country's citizens through democratic elections. The nation-state may have come to the West very much later than in China. But the Western nation-state is vastly superior to that of China thanks to the rule of law and electoral democracy, even if Western democracy is struggling somewhat today.

How long China's anachronistic political situation can persist is a big question. Today, the CCP is visibly worried, as is evident from the growing repression, surveillance, use of propaganda, and nationalism. The political crisis in Hong Kong shows the limitations of authoritarianism. Any political instability and possible regime change in China would certainly have a massive impact on the world, and especially on Australia.

John West

Richard McGregor

In Peter Hartcher's telling, Australia has undergone an epiphany over China in the past two to three years. Politicians of all stripes, sections of the academy, the media and the bureaucracy have at different times woken up to the fact that China is much more than a valuable economic partner for Australia. Rather, the country has emerged as something more formidable: a uniquely powerful party-state that fuses ordinary diplomatic relations with a determination to ensure any interaction with foreigners buttresses communist rule in China.

Hartcher accurately describes the genesis of Beijing's interference campaigns, something too few observers manage to do. Beijing's efforts to influence Australian politics by fair means and foul started as defensive in nature. Beijing wants to make sure that the hundreds of thousands of mainland migrants and students in Australia don't become carriers of a democratic virus that can be transported back into China.

In some respects, it has succeeded. The Chinese community in Australia is very diverse. Some have been here for decades. Others have just landed or gained citizenship. They are rich, poor and middle class and work in the private and public sectors. They don't vote along party lines. They have different religions – Buddhism, Catholism and evangelical Christianity – and often no religion at all.

The most prominent and powerful community organisations and Chinese-language media, by contrast, are nearly all pro-Beijing and allergic to criticising the CCP. That's not by accident. If you criticise the CCP in Australia, the party can make sure your business or relatives pay a price in China, and perhaps in Australia as well, where the community can be mobilised on Beijing's behalf.

However, once people wise up to how the party-state works, the gains that the CCP makes in strengthening its rule at home start to evaporate abroad. The backlash against China that Hartcher describes is not confined to Australia. It is happening across the developed world, and in many developing nations as well.

The backlash is by no means universal. Chinese investment is welcome in many countries, from Asia to Africa. Nor is all the criticism necessarily fair in every circumstance. China's conflict with the reigning superpower, the United States, is multifaceted – covering trade, economics, geopolitics and ideology. But it is also about raw power. Superpowers like the US do not give way without a fight.

That is one of the conundrums in analysing China's rise. The challenges posed by Beijing do not always arise from the fact that China is pursuing nefarious ends. They also come because China is behaving just as any great state would. It wants to dominate the Indo-Pacific, and, over time, push the United States out of the region. To be sure, Beijing is doing so through absurd territorial claims in the South China Sea, which are being enforced through intimidation of neighbouring Southeast Asian nations. But China would be challenging the United States no matter what kind of government was in power in Beijing.

Hartcher lays out with precision how the China landscape has been transformed in Australia. China's interests go well beyond managing the politics of the Australian Chinese community and Chinese student population. Australia's alliance with the United States, the trade and business relationship, our intelligence assets and foreign policy – all are under pressure. In addition, Canberra, like other governments, has to deal with the extra-territorial demands of the party-state. Beijing aims to condition foreign governments and politicians to internalise its own talking points on issues like Taiwan and the South China Sea, to the point where our policies all but match China's.

While Hartcher depicts the China threat very well, I think he underplays the other side of this equation: how to manage the opportunities in the relationship. Put another way, Australia has an anti-China policy, but it has yet to develop a comprehensive China policy, one which is strategic in protecting Australia's long-term interests but sly and adept enough to take advantage of any benefits that the bilateral relationship throws up.

When I say "anti-China," I don't mean that in a pejorative sense, although the term is often used that way. A once-in-a-generation about-turn on an issue as momentous as China was always going to provoke intense debate and personal rancour. That is certainly the case in Australia, where taking any position on an issue relating to China can immediately see you tattooed by critics on the other side of the argument as being in one camp or another for life. And heaven forbid you call for more nuance in the debate. Nuance, in the eyes of some, has become a byword for appeasement. The bitter, binary split over China undercuts any efforts to find common ground.

As Hartcher hints at, rightly in my view, Australia has to learn how to walk and chew gum at the same time. There is nothing wrong with taking a tougher political line on China while also trying to protect the significant economic relationship. Japan, and to a lesser extent Singapore, have done a much better job at this. Why can't Australia?

It is all very well to talk about diversifying our trading ties, as many do, but it is not so easy in practice. We also forget that trade and investment with China is a two-way street. Australia too often describes itself as reliant on China, which immediately puts our governing class into a defensive crouch. A more confident country would see itself as interdependent. The trade relationship is important for another reason that the defence and national security hawks don't like to talk about. They might ask themselves how they are going to fund bigger military budgets while simultaneously scaling back business ties with China. As grating as it might have been, Beijing's ambassador, Cheng Jingye, was right when he said at the end of 2019 that Australia's trade and budget surpluses were built on the back of trade with China.

It is hard to be too critical of Hartcher for not sketching out in detail how a better relationship with China might unfold. There are so many variables: Chinese internal politics; how Beijing's ties with the United States in particular, but also Japan and south-east Asian nations, evolve; how far China pushes its defence interests in the Pacific, where Australia has so much at stake; whether India can reach its economic potential and act as a counterbalance to China. There is no telling the future in the region.

Still, on two of Hartcher's recommendations, I disagree. The first is his recommendation that MPs should submit to formal security clearance. Security vetting takes months at a minimum. In the case of Chinese Australians joining the bureaucracy, ASIO not only screens their relatives in Australia, but also in China. To understand how disastrous this could be in practice, imagine how such a scenario might have played out in the last federal election. If Labor had won a few more seats, the result could have hung on Liberal Gladys Liu's election in Chisholm, in Melbourne. Leaving aside how fraught, impractical and inefficient a vetting process would be, the question of which party would govern Australia could have been left hanging on ASIO's assessment of one candidate's loyalty. Further, ASIO could refuse to issue a security clearance, and then decline to say why. Australia's intelligence agencies have been enthusiastic partners with the government in the expansion of the security state in recent years. But even Duncan Lewis, the outgoing ASIO chief, disavowed this suggestion. Far better, I think, to leave such vetting to the political process, the media and the parties themselves, and to have it all done in public. The voters can then make up their own minds.

The second is Hartcher's idea that ethnic Chinese be favoured as immigrants over applicants from mainland China itself. This sets up a dangerous slippery slope, in my view. We have no data, for a start, telling us about the political views of mainland migrants as opposed to those from, say, Taiwan, Singapore or Malaysia. Many mainlanders, like Feng Chongyi, whom Hartcher interviews for his essay, love Australia precisely because it is a democracy. Are mainland Chinese to be put through some higher-level loyalty test before they are accepted as migrants? How would this be administered? Should applicants from the mainland be excluded because they credit the Communist Party for their country's economic advances over recent decades? Where else in the world should this test be applied? Do we allow in Indians who back Narendra Modi's anti-Muslim policies? Should we have had stricter tests for Serbians, after the last Balkan conflict, to see which side they were on?

After Australia discarded the White Australia policy, one of the strengths of its immigration system has been that it is non-discriminatory. Maybe that has slipped here and there (for example, recently, in favouring Iraqi Christians for entry over Muslims from that region), but this is not something we should encourage, as politicians will find endless ways to slice and dice and weaponise the criteria for entry. In a successful multicultural country, there is a lot at stake.

The emphasis should be on what Hartcher correctly advocates elsewhere in his essay: the proper enforcement of the foreign interference laws that were passed in 2018 but have barely been enforced since. If our democratic processes, political parties, institutions and civil society are resilient and in good order, we wouldn't have to canvass policies like this.

Richard McGregor

Correspondence

Henry Sherrell

Peter Hartcher's essay is a timely call to action about the Chinese Communist Party's intentions for Australia. He outlines a host of decisions collectively awaiting Australia, and raises the prospect of a more difficult future, where economic and security trade-offs are more explicit. The brazen nature of the intimidation he describes is particularly concerning. This is a conversation worth having. Yet a detour into Australian immigration policy shows how easily it can go off-track.

Nearly three in ten Australian residents were born overseas. Yet in public debates like this one, immigration policy is often treated as a pawn on a chessboard – something small to be sacrificed for a larger purpose. Hartcher's essay is only the most recent example of this phenomenon.

Hartcher calls for civil society and governments to do more to educate "immigrants and the wider community alike on the value of democracy and the responsibilities of citizens." It is hard to argue with this proposal, though such efforts often go awry in clumsy execution. He calls for better-qualified officials to assess prospective immigrants more closely. Finally, he suggests the introduction of some form of values test, as "immigrants who are committed to liberal-democratic principles should always be given priority over those who are not." This is not a new concept. Speaking in the federal parliamentary debate on the *Immigration Restriction Act* in 1901, James Ronald MP said, "Let us tell these foreign races that when they can live up to our social and moral ideals we shall welcome them."

Like many areas of public policy, the administration of immigration policy is not straightforward. Assessing visa applications is different to looking for contaminated food during quarantine screening. No government official can peer into someone's soul and understand their true intentions. In particular, the introduction of a formal liberal-democratic values test in the immigration selection process would generate extreme difficulties. What would an objective test for commitment to liberal-democratic values look like? How would an official from the Department of Home Affairs assess this test in relation to individual visa applications?

Instead of buttressing Australia's liberal democracy, such a test would undermine it. A values test would be impossible to assess without considering where people come from. Despite our aspirations to non-discrimination, where people hail from remains a core criterion shaping Australian immigration policy. A British tourist has no difficulty coming to Australia, but ask an Afghan or Indian citizen about the process and you will find it beset with hurdles. Yet the CCP, not to mention many migrants, would view an Australian values test for immigration selection as a proxy for race. It is worth recalling that under White Australia, migrants were not ostensibly excluded on the grounds of race, but of language.

Hartcher is not racist, nor is he "anti-Chinese." He explicitly argues for additional immigration from Taiwan and Hong Kong. In the past, he has articulated support for a larger Australian population, which will increasingly depend primarily on Asian and African immigration. But in a country that was federated in part on anti-Asian prejudice and is now home to a large and growing Asian-Australian population, we are compelled to take perceptions of our actions seriously.

How would citizens from countries like the Philippines, Vietnam and Pakistan successfully showcase their commitment to liberal-democratic principles? These are people Hartcher would welcome with open arms. Yet these people also live in countries governed by non-democratic or illiberal regimes. Alongside mainland China and India, they are among the largest recent migrant cohorts to Australia.

For almost all immigrants to Australia, the act of migration itself is a vote for our liberal democracy. There is no evidence to suggest the vast majority of migrants from these countries are undermining Australia's political system. If anything, it is the opposite. The 2015 report *Australians Today* found people born in China and Hong Kong who had migrated to Australia between 2001 and 2014 were more likely than recent migrants from New Zealand to feel a sense of belonging in Australia. And they were just as likely to feel that sense of belonging as recent British-born migrants. Those fleeing authoritarianism – people born in Iraq, Afghanistan or Iran – had the most sense of belonging of any group. Like Cold War Soviet émigrés, those who have lived under authoritarian regimes may become the loudest supporters of their new home.

This points to alternative means for addressing the threats Hartcher details. As he argues forcefully, Australian governments and civil society can and must do better to strengthen ourselves against active interference from the CCP. Given the existing, almost limitless powers granted to the Minister for Immigration, directing resources to cancel visas through ministerial discretion is likely to be more effective than empty screening devices such as a values test. We would also do well to consider existing policy directions – such as the ongoing privatisation of parts of the visa application process – and ask what risks this may pose for future Australian capacity to assess threats. Boiled down, visa privatisation is an example of the trade-offs presciently outlined by Hartcher: more fiscal operating space at the expense of poorer oversight and administrative control.

Finally, Hartcher's immigration proposal shrinks from the promise of Australia. By rebalancing immigration opportunities away from people who may not share a strong affinity for liberal democracy before they get here, he dismisses the prospect that living in Australia can itself foster liberal-democratic values. His proposal fails to consider how the idea of Australia, the very values we seek to protect, can influence those who move here. This is the strongest argument for immigration as a nation-building enterprise, where we engage newcomers by the lived commitment of all Australians, old and new, to our shared liberal-democratic values.

To counter the rising authoritarianism of this political moment, we must socialise our values through our actions. As well as asking hard questions about a host of other immigration policy decisions, this means refusing to judge prospective Australian immigrants' commitment to liberal democracy by the actions and worldview of regimes such as the CCP.

Henry Sherrell

Wanning Sun

On my first reading of Peter Hartcher's *Red Flag*, the following passage leapt out at me:

> In other words, we understand that you have ties of sentiment and bonds of kinship to other countries, and we're unconcerned. We know it takes time to put down roots in new social soil. This is part of democratic pluralism and it's an enrichment of a society. But the nation cannot tolerate acts to advance a foreign political movement with hostile intentions.

Further on, Hartcher recommends that the Australian government should consider "changing the composition [of Australia's immigration profile] in favour of Chinese immigrants from places other than mainland China." He says: "Screening must still apply, of course, but prima facie ethnic Chinese immigrants from Taiwan or Hong Kong are more likely to value Australian liberties ... preference should not only be given to immigrants with the most suitable work skills but also to those with the most compatible values." This would, Hartcher argues, "improve the balance of risks."

Let's examine the logic of this argument. Hartcher says that People's Republic of China migrants are a risk. I assume he reached that conclusion, at least partly, through his own observations of the actions and behaviour of PRC migrants in Australia. Or was it based mainly on the claims made by Professor Feng Chongyi? Perhaps he received an undisclosed briefing from ASIO that provided some concrete evidence to substantiate the public assertions made by retired ASIO head Duncan Lewis – whom Hartcher quotes approvingly? Hartcher leaves us to speculate about the factual basis for his fears – fears so grave he advocates a discriminatory change to our immigration policy in regards to our largest trading partner, the birthplace of our largest non-Anglo migrant population. Assume, for a moment, that there is some factual, moral and political cogency to his argument, and that in response the Australian government decides not to accept any further migrants from the PRC. What should the government do with the half a million PRC migrants who are already naturalised Australian citizens?

Given that PRC migrants come from a country with "hostile intentions," as Hartcher puts it, and given that their past, current or possible future behaviour is apparently of sufficient concern that Hartcher wants to "armour-plate" (he used this phrase in an interview with Tom Switzer) Australia against any risks posed by them and their homeland, the logical and most urgent thing to do would be to take measures against them. Surely these PRC migrants already in Australia are a more credible and imminent threat than any future PRC migrants, who, in the current climate, would come under intense scrutiny during the screening process – even without an outright ban on PRC immigration. Shouldn't Hartcher be urging the government to take a leaf out of China's own playbook – or Australia's wartime internment playbook – and consider putting them all into detention or "re-education" camps, as China does with the Uighurs? But what would you do with the thousands of non-Chinese Australians who have married PRC migrants, not to mention the thousands of children these PRC migrants have produced? How many generations of "distance" from the PRC would they need to demonstrate before qualifying as politically trustworthy? At a minimum, and drawing instead on George Orwell, shouldn't our domestic intelligence organisations implement widespread and personalised surveillance of all PRC migrants and their close associates – if they haven't done so already – just to play it safe? This, of course, would be an excellent justification for a vast increase in funding for these organisations. If China is to be treated *seriously* as a country with hostile intentions – rather than just being a sacrificial pawn in a game of rhetorical brinkmanship – then the logic of Hartcher's argument seems to lead him ineluctably down such a path.

Max Suich, a former chief editorial executive of Fairfax, recently observed in a letter to the editor of *The Sydney Morning Herald* that "The conspiratorial material, unsourced, that often purports to document the Chinese threat, can only come, directly or indirectly from the intelligence community's conduits and media handlers." Suich further observed that "these 'scoops' have made the threat the dominant theme in discussion of relations with China in what is the liberal wing of the Australian media, which might usually be expected to be a bit more sceptical about the actual dimensions of the threat."

Like Suich, I'm baffled why the left and the right have become such odd bedfellows on this issue. Does it not intrigue or bother Hartcher, as a senior journalist of the "liberal wing of the Australian media," that he seems to be singing from the same song sheet as Andrew Bolt on the topic of China and Chinese influence?

I think I understand – up to a point. Hartcher abhors communism, and he's wary – no, extremely worried – that China is seeking to infiltrate the so-called free world. He's keen to see that our democratic values stay constant and strong. He wants to find a way to minimise the likelihood of Australia and the Australian way of life being jeopardised by China's current and future actions. And many PRC migrants would support him in that; that's why they're here, not in China. However, if Australia halted immigration from the PRC without presenting any evidence that many – or even any – of these potential migrants harbour "hostile intentions" towards Australia, this would imply a profound lack of confidence in the effectiveness of our security and intelligence agencies in screening potential migrants. And if that's the case, then how can we rely on them to screen potential migrants from other nations? Shouldn't we just pull up the drawbridge on immigration altogether?

Hartcher cites Huang Xiangmo as an example of a Chinese person who was a "covert agent of influence for the CCP" within Australia. But even if Huang had been brought to trial and found guilty of the accusations against him, it remains true that the vast majority of PRC migrants in Australia do not act in these ways. So my question to Hartcher is this: what does a PRC migrant or permanent resident in Australia have to do in order to be exempted from his suspicion – given that Hartcher stops short of using ethnic Chineseness as his criterion for discrimination? If Hartcher is reluctant to go down the path of internment camps for former citizens of a country suspected of having "hostile intentions" towards Australia, then what would he count as proof of their loyalty to Australia, in order to justify allowing them to continue going about their lives as normal?

It may be useful for Hartcher to know a few things about how pro-China patriotism works. First, the love that many PRC migrants harbour for their homeland is not exclusively the handiwork of the CCP. If Hartcher believes that, he's giving the CCP and its propaganda apparatus far too much credit. It's the market: nationalism sells. And the internet: nationalism can be clickbait. And it's also simply the sense of oneness that we humans seem almost inevitably disposed to feel towards the culture we are born into and the people who nurture us; even from an evolutionary point of view, nationalism looks like a useful default position. Finally, Hartcher should realise that journalists such as he may unintentionally lend a helping hand to the CCP in advancing its ideological work within Australia, by effectively pushing many migrants closer to "the other side."

There seems to be a huge blind spot in the narrative of the "untrustworthy PRC diaspora": modern China has experienced only one-party rule. These migrants, and those who remain in China, did not choose to live in a communist country. They were born into that system. It's not that there's the CCP and one or more opposition parties, and that Chinese people have chosen to side with the CCP. It's not only unfair but also illogical to assume that citizens of the PRC – or PRC migrants – are loyal to the CCP simply because they live, or have lived, in a nation ruled by that party.

I lead a research team, funded by an Australian Research Council Discovery Projects grant, investigating the cultural practices of PRC Chinese communities in Australia and their use of Chinese-language social media. We have published some of these findings in peer-reviewed journals, and while our research is ongoing we're already convinced that this is an extremely heterogeneous cohort, marked by great diversity in class background, education level and cosmopolitanism, as well as in their political distance from the PRC. We've conducted large-scale surveys, in-depth interviews and longitudinal ethnographic research. Our findings suggest that PRC migrants don't always side with the Chinese government on matters of political policy (just as non-Chinese Australians don't always side with the Australian government). Most of our survey respondents were very happy to promote Australia and many of them were already actively doing so. Our careful analysis of the content of Australia's Chinese-language media suggests that it is not functioning merely as a blunt and unquestioning tool of the Chinese government and its state media, nor is it just a ventriloquist for mainstream English-language media. Rather, wedged between a frequently anti-Chinese public rhetoric in Australia's mainstream media and anti-Australian responses in China's state media, Chinese-language media in Australia seems to profit by giving voice to PRC migrants' sense of ambivalence towards both Australia and China. Our engaged ethnographic interaction with more than forty WeChat groups of first-generation PRC migrants indicates they have a very high desire to learn about democratic values, practices and processes.

Throughout the summer months, as Australia's bushfires burned, I closely followed how PRC Chinese migrants used WeChat to organise fundraising events and mobilise fellow citizens to make donations for bushfire victims; how they spread stories about volunteer firefighters of Chinese heritage and about generous and compassionate non-Chinese Aussies; and how they engaged in heated debate on the relationship between climate change and bushfires. Their reason for doing these things was simple: as one Chinese community organisation put it, "Australia is our home."

Democracy is Australia's biggest soft-power asset, and we must work hard to keep it. But if you start to think, talk and behave like an authoritarian government, and start to distrust your own citizens and question the allegiance of PRC migrants on the basis of the actions of a few individuals, then you are taking a crucial step towards undermining the "brand" of Australia as a liberal democracy and effectively shooting yourself in the foot. That's certainly not the way to "armour-plate" Australia.

Finally, in an excellent piece Hartcher wrote recently on Scott Morrison's lack of leadership, he says:

> Populism – of the left and the right – is a political style offering unworkably simplistic solutions to complex problems . . . Our leaders do not single out Muslims or Mexicans or other minorities for special exclusion. Our leaders do not risk national breakup by sponsoring divisive shocks, like the one now testing the unity of the United Kingdom.

Here, Hartcher appears to be arguing directly against the position he articulated in his Quarterly Essay, where he urged our leaders to single out prospective PRC migrants – literally – for special exclusion. There, he appeared unconcerned that his position amounted to an unworkably simplistic and seemingly populist solution to a deeply complex problem. Following the logic of his own argument, can we assume that Hartcher now wants to recant the position he advanced in *Red Flag*?

Wanning Sun

Caroline Rosenberg

As an early product of the infamous one-child policy, and now a proud Melburnian, I read Peter Hartcher's essay with mixed feelings. Despite twenty years of introspective reconciliation, I still struggle to process all the contradictions that come with being a migrant from communist China to democratic Australia.

In China I wore the red scarf in primary school as a symbol that I was part of the Young Pioneers of China – so did every student in every school I knew of. Like Aussie kids wearing the scarf of the AFL team their family has always supported, we wore our scarves proudly, though you could argue that neither Aussie nor Chinese kids have much say in the matter. We were taught how great the Communist party is, how it liberated the whole of China, and how corruptible capitalism is, with little children getting paid only a dollar a day to work in mines. I was quite happy that I didn't have to work in mines, and that my parents loved only me.

Within my first week of school in Australia, on a bus ride, I overheard someone say, "Chairman Mao was a dictator, he killed millions in China." I had to look up what a dictator was, discreetly, on my little handheld electronic translator. Nowadays, with smartphones, it would be much easier to be inconspicuous, but this was 1999. I was horrified by the stupidity, absurdity and audacity of someone making such a statement in public. Surely, I, a real Chinese person from China, would know if someone had killed millions of people in my own country. I concluded that the ignorant speaker had never been to China, had never seen the massive portrait of Mao at Tiananmen. But I was tremendously curious that no one else on the bus seemed bothered by the inflammatory conversation. Like a good child of the Middle Kingdom, a follower of the Middle Way, I withheld my burning desire to protest. Mainly because I couldn't construct grammatically correct and fluent sentences in English, even in my head, yet. Really. It had nothing to do with being a coward.

I often reflect on that twenty-minute bus ride. The waves of China's past caught up with me steadily, piling up without any regard for my psychological well-being. I learnt the realities of the Tiananmen Square massacre, the "liberation" of Tibet and Xinjiang, the real horror behind the Great Leap Forward, the Cultural Revolution, abandoned baby girls and "prevented births." This new knowledge hit me head-on at the beginning of the new millennium. I was one of millions of international students from China seeking a better education in the West. I'm sure I wasn't the only one who struggled to make sense of right and wrong, good and evil, as we digested this information. Degrees, promotions and mortgages helped with day-to-day orientation in Australia. Mostly, I assimilated and pushed on. Really. Life keeps getting in the way, and who has the time to question and make sense of these big issues? It's not that I am a coward.

Reading Hartcher's call to action, where he quotes former ASIO chief Duncan Lewis saying that Chinese Australians "could and should" be "vital" in protecting Australia's democracy, I did a little celebration dance inside. I was excited to read on. But the Chinese Australian community did not feature again in the essay as part of the solution. Instead, Hartcher argued they needed to be educated more about democratic values, and assisted to participate fully in their new democracy. I recognise the importance of macro strategies, broad strokes. I wish someone had given me Hartcher's essay when I arrived in Australia as a teenager. I don't mean that literally, of course, as I didn't know much English at the time and I couldn't have cared less about politics. But I wish I'd had a crash course, an overview, like Hartcher's essay, on how Australians and the West view communism, China and the Chinese. I knew how I viewed the West, but I was utterly unprepared for how it views me. This reverse shock is not dissimilar to the shock that Hartcher describes Joe Hockey and the Labor trio going through. I recognise that it is irrational and unreasonable to expect one essay by one journalist to have all the answers, especially when it is clearly titled: *Red Flag: Waking up to China's challenge*, not *Green Light: Working Solutions for China's Challenge*. As a Chinese Australian, I am grateful for the essay. I may not have read it the way the author intended, and I am ashamed of my disappointment. What have I done in twenty years? I have mixed feelings.

But to return to the idea that we should stand up for ourselves, I wonder if Hartcher would mind standing with the Chinese-looking Australians? Would he be intimidated if there were too many Chinese-looking Australians around him? Would he wonder if these Chinese-looking Australians were spies? Or comrades? Would he trust Chinese Australians, amphibians of the two cultures, never to lose sight of our democratic values? Would he ever see Chinese Australians as individuals – intelligent individuals, the way he sees Ross and John Garnaut? I am curious. Even a coward can be curious.

I can construct proper sentences now, grammatically correct and fluent for the most part. I can't change the fact that I was born a Chinese single child, but I choose to sip a Magic (a distinctly Melburnian coffee with a perfectly balanced ratio of coffee and milk) every morning and cheer for the Pies in my black and white scarf once in a while. Whenever Chinese Australians are asked to choose between China and Australia, the ultimate answer must be that we choose humanity.

Caroline Rosenberg

Correspondence

Sam Roggeveen

By the time Peter Hartcher released his Quarterly Essay in late November 2019, Australia's China debate had reached a point of near hysteria. The suggestion, made on *60 Minutes*, that China's security services had tried to cultivate an aspiring Liberal Party MP who later died mysteriously was leapt upon by China hawks eager to confirm their biases. Days later, *The Australian* described a fairly routine reorganisation of the bureaucracy as evidence that our spy agencies were on a "war footing" against Chinese interference in Australia's politics.

In the circumstances, the core message of Hartcher's essay was a useful one: Australia can do this. It is well within our powers as a nation, Hartcher argues, to maintain our sovereignty and the integrity of our democratic institutions. He's right, of course. After all, this is not entirely new territory for Australia, given the espionage threat we faced from the Soviet bloc in the Cold War. Granted, the locus of Soviet espionage and subversion was Europe; Australia was on the periphery. Now we are nearer the centre. But we know from the European example that it is possible for smaller nations to withstand such pressure from a great power.

Yet considering the overall China challenge, I can't help thinking Hartcher has put too much weight on this serious but manageable portion of the problem – that is, foreign influence. Meeting the China challenge will be more difficult than Hartcher allows, because he underestimates both the scale of China's rise and the depth of Australia's political malaise.

The reason the scale of China's challenge is so important is that it will determine whether or not our ally the United States will meet it. Hartcher doesn't consider the possibility that Washington might choose *not* to compete with China. While he closes his essay with a stirring call for Australia to strengthen itself because we "cannot count on anyone else," he also repeatedly emphasises the importance of the US alliance to Australia. In other words, his argument is largely premised on the idea that we *can* count on someone else.

Yes, the alliance is, as Hartcher puts it, a "national asset," but it is a diminishing one. Hartcher admits that the United States is becoming less reliable, but he attributes this almost entirely to President Trump. Unfortunately, the problem goes much deeper than that. The US has never faced an adversary of superior economic strength, until now. So if it is going to resist China's leadership ambitions, its motivation had better be really strong. After all, we're talking about a multi-generational, whole-of-government contest against a power that, in economic terms, dwarfs the Soviet Union.

Yet if the United States is serious about such a contest, we have seen little sign of it. Yes, Trump has imposed tariffs, and China has been designated a "strategic competitor." But America's military presence in Asia has remained largely unchanged in the past two decades despite a vast increase in China's military strength. America's major Asian economic initiative, the Trans-Pacific Partnership, died at the hands of Trump. And if America was truly committed to a contest that will be harder than that against the Soviets, wouldn't the US president have addressed the nation on such an important topic by now? Wouldn't he have used the State of the Union or a nationally televised statement to inspire his people for the struggle ahead?

We shouldn't be surprised that these things have not happened. The United States isn't under economic threat from China because it's not in Beijing's interests to lock the US out of Asia economically, even if it can do so strategically. And the US isn't at direct military risk either, because as strong as China is becoming, it will always be hemmed in by other great powers in Asia – India, Japan and Russia in the first instance, and in future perhaps a unified Korea as well as Indonesia, should it fulfil its potential.

But although these countries will ensure that China never entirely dominates Asia, none can prevent Beijing from becoming its leading power, and none of them will replace the US as a security partner for Australia. So Hartcher is more right than he knows: Australia is likely to be alone, with no one else to count on. We had better prepare, and Hartcher makes a number of recommendations for how we can do so.

However, his proposal to have security agencies vet serving MPs and senators, and anyone standing for office at upcoming elections, is unconvincing. Why assume the security agencies are any better at spotting threats than the voters, given the breaches Australia has suffered in recent decades (remember Jean-Philippe Wispelaere and Simon Lappas?) and KGB penetration of ASIO during the Cold War?

Nor does Hartcher's idea of a bipartisan "strategic council" to reconcile party differences on China policy offer much hope, mainly because the parties themselves are so hopeless. Both are in secular decline. In a rapidly growing population, their membership base is shrinking, and at the last election both suffered a falling primary vote, reinforcing a decades-long trend. The vast majority of Australians care nothing for our two big parties, yet the parties maintain their place at the centre of politics, thanks largely to a favourable voting system.

It is worth recalling that Australia's party-political structure was completely redefined by the Cold War. The Liberal Party had anti-communism in its DNA from its earliest days, even taking Australia to a referendum on the issue in 1951. The Labor Party split over communism and spent the 1960s and much of the '70s in Opposition as a result. It didn't win office during the Cold War until the breach was healed, and only had a sustained period in government when it found an unambiguously pro-American leader in Bob Hawke.

Given that the rise of China is a much bigger deal for Australia than the Soviet Union ever was, and given also that our two major parties have never commanded less public authority and esteem than they do today, why would we assume they are well placed to navigate the formidable challenges ahead?

Neither party has the energy or the resolve to confront the idea that Australia is likely to be left alone in a region in which China is the leading power. For Australia to meet that challenge, the major parties will either need to redefine themselves as they did in the Cold War, or make way.

Sam Roggeveen

Peter Hartcher

It might be intended as a rhetorical question, but I'm going to answer it anyway, because it is vital and urgent. In her response to my essay, Caroline Rosenberg sets out some of the complexities of growing up as a Chinese Australian. She writes, "But to return to the idea that we should stand up for ourselves, I wonder if Hartcher would mind standing with the Chinese-looking Australians?"

I do not mind. On the contrary, I gladly, firmly stand with Chinese Australians.

Caroline, you and the other 1.3 million Chinese Australians are an asset to our country. You are also part of a community under unique stress, and needing unique support from the rest of the country. It is a fundamental test of Australia's national cohesion.

The Chinese Communist Party has put you in an invidious position. The party claims the unswerving loyalty of Chinese people. It is a political claim, yet staked on the basis of biology. And so even when you leave China, choose to live in another country, make that country your home, conceive children there, take up citizenship there, Xi Jinping demands your loyalty to an authoritarian political project in another land.

Of course, the CCP doesn't present it as a political matter. The party has long conflated itself with the Chinese nation, Chinese ethnicity and Chinese civilisation. But Beijing demands not just a gesture of affection or acknowledgement of Chinese civilisation. It insists on your support for the policies of this administration. Worse, Xi demands it as a higher duty than any loyalty to your adopted country. Even if you've never lived in China, even if you and your family have chosen another land, other loyalties, generations ago.

Australia has lots of experience with immigrants who retain residual attachments to their homelands. Such attachments are normal and natural. Australia has no objection to these, and shouldn't have. But when a foreign power makes a demand on the "flesh and blood" ties of its diaspora, in the phrase emphasised by the Chinese government's United Front Work Department, to infringe on the freedoms and rights of Australians, that is a red line.

Kevin Rudd has called the CCP "the enemy of liberal democracy." It works to advance its values and policies in Australia through hundreds of front groups. Some, like the Confucius Institutes and Confucius Classrooms, have more obvious ties to the Chinese government. Others, masquerading as community associations, business chambers, campus associations or patriotic societies, are less identifiable, even though organised through the covert activity of Beijing's United Front Work Department.

Professor Feng Chongyi of the University of Technology Sydney counts more than 300 such associations active in Sydney alone, and hundreds more across the country. These groups commonly put pressure on Chinese Australians to carry out political tasks for Beijing, undermining Australian values and interests in the process.

These Chinese Australians need support from Australia to resist such pressure. And they need help in upholding what many have pledged in becoming citizens: their "loyalty to Australia and its people, whose democratic beliefs I share, whose rights and liberties I respect, and whose laws I will uphold and obey." Until now, they have not had any support in facing these pernicious pressures. The rest of Australia has been oblivious to their quiet dilemmas and private struggles.

The Foreign Influence Transparency Scheme and the espionage and foreign interference laws passed by Australia's parliament in 2017 were designed to make a start by unmasking these groups and curbing their activities. But the laws were hollow. The government did not provide the money, the staff or the political will to enforce them.

Since my Quarterly Essay was published, two things have changed. First, the Morrison government has announced that it is allocating $40 million to enforce the laws. So that should supply the money and the staff. And the political will? We will know that they are serious when we start seeing arrests and expulsions. Second, the COVID-19 epidemic broke out. This epidemic is making many Chinese Australians feel isolated and disdained by the rest of the country. This is precisely the opposite of what they need to feel – that they are a valued part of the community – and precisely the opposite of what Australia needs to preserve its national cohesion and social harmony.

Some leaders have led. For instance, Queensland's premier, Annastacia Palaszczuk, and Sydney's Lord Mayor, Clover Moore, were quick and visible in joining Chinese New Year celebrations and expressing solidarity with their Chinese Australian communities. They lent support and countered fear-mongering.

Weeks later, Scott Morrison expressed the right sentiments in parliament. He stated that Chinese Australians "deserve our great appreciation and support." Labor's Anthony Albanese did the same. Both leaders could and should do much more: visiting Australia's various Chinatowns mask-free, consistent with their own health advisories, and sitting down to yum cha; embracing the Chinese Australian community; making speeches in support.

It is a moment of great stress for the Chinese Australian community, and a great opportunity for the rest of Australia to help ease that stress. All Australia's political, business and community leaders should stand with the "Chinese-looking Australians," Caroline, in the national tradition of looking after our fellow Australians when they suffer adversity. And they should be doing this even as the authorities seek to disrupt the CCP's covert efforts to press the Chinese Australian community to serve a foreign authoritarian project to undermine our sovereignty.

The Chinese Australian community is an asset that must be protected; the Chinese Communist Party is a liability that must be constrained.

And Caroline, you pose a question about attitudes to communism. Please allow me to point out that communism is not really the issue here. China is not the only communist party–ruled regional state with a large Australian connection. Vietnam, formally the Socialist Republic of Vietnam, is ruled by an authoritarian Marxist–Leninist party. Australia is home to a substantial Vietnamese-Australian community: about a quarter of a million people. Yet there is no tension here. Because Vietnam's government is not making systematic efforts to lay claim to the loyalties of the Vietnamese-Australian community. It is not organising the covert penetration of Australian politics. It is not attempting to subvert Australia's freedoms.

The federal government has dramatically elevated diplomatic relations with Vietnam over the past couple of years. Relations are flourishing. Communism as a movement or an ideology is neither necessary nor sufficient to pose a threat to Australia's sovereignty. The risk stems from the policy and strategy of a specific political organisation, namely the CCP, bent on domination of its neighbourhood, and not any stripe of political ideology in itself.

To Amy King, I have not so much an answer as a question. Are you feeling lucky? Because you are essentially rationalising Australian inaction in the face of China's challenge. In doing so, you ignore every sign of Beijing's organised, determined program to take control of Australia's decision-makers.

You draw attention to my case studies of attempted CCP intrusion into Australian politics – the cases involving Joe Hockey, Stephen Conroy, Bill Shorten, Penny Wong and Richard Marles. You observe, correctly, that all these attempts failed. And conclude that I am therefore disregarding my own evidence when I urge Australia to better protect its democracy against such interference. But this is to misunderstand. I cite these examples to show that the party's intrusions are very real, very bold and very high-level. We are not jumping at shadows. Beijing is waging a concerted effort to gain as much influence as possible over our political leaders. We know about these cases because they failed: principled Australian politicians rejected Beijing's overtures. And because those patriots were affronted by the Chinese government's actions, they alerted their colleagues. That's how we know of these incidents. But how many successful efforts has Beijing made? These are the ones we don't hear about – where threats or inducements are quietly accepted, and the Chinese government gets its way. With a wide-open system of political donations, desperately cash-hungry politicians and no federal anti-corruption body, our system is wide open.

The successful intrusions are the ones we will probably only wake up to long after they've succeeded. As the former Hong Kong chief secretary Anson Chan warns, "By the time China's infiltration of Australia is readily apparent, it will be too late."

And Amy, you are right, of course, that China's diplomacy is often ham-fisted and counterproductive. The CCP is not infallible. But if you look at the broad trajectory of China's growing power and influence over the past forty years, you would have to be feeling very lucky indeed to punt that it will stop here and go no further. If we sit inert waiting for China to fail, we surrender control pre-emptively.

You argue that what Australia really needs is an overarching China strategy. Of course it does. But this doesn't mean we should do nothing until our leaders manage to produce one. We could be waiting an awfully long time, and time is not our friend with this problem.

Similarly, Sam Roggeveen thinks that it's pointless to try to protect ourselves until we achieve a precondition, but an even bigger one: "For Australia to meet that challenge, the major parties will either need to redefine themselves as they did in the Cold War, or make way." Can we really afford to wait for a wholesale reorganisation of our political system before we deal with an urgent challenge to our sovereignty?

Other correspondents also make the case for inaction. David Walker may be right that climate change is the bigger problem. Yet even if this is accurate, it is also irrelevant. Surely we must deal with both?

The responses to my essay have changed my mind on one important recommendation. David Walker, together with others, including Richard McGregor and Sam Roggeveen, have persuaded me to modify my proposal that Australia needs to subject new MPs and senators to security vetting. I still maintain that they do need to be vetted. In discussing this idea in a range of forums, from talkback radio to university seminars, I discovered that most Australians assume that this happens already as a matter of course. They are shocked to learn it does not. And, in conducting the Sydney launch for the essay, Julie Bishop agreed that a security screening was necessary for federal lawmakers. But where I suggested ASIO could do the security screening, I've subsequently been convinced that this isn't the best approach. Because it would make the domestic intelligence agency the gatekeeper to Australia's democracy.

The better way, I propose, is to create an independent parliamentary office to run security checks on new MPs and senators, and to do so at the candidate stage. Set up as a parliamentary agency, it would be accountable to the parliament itself. We have a precedent, though in a different realm of expertise. The Parliamentary Budget Office was created in 2012 to make expert, non-partisan costings of the political parties' budget proposals. Why did we need this? Because we'd learnt that we couldn't trust our politicians to be honest about the true cost of their election promises. This problem had dogged every election campaign for decades and confused the electorate. The Parliamentary Budget Office, well regarded by all political parties, solved the problem.

We should set up an independent, non-partisan parliamentary agency along the same lines to examine the backgrounds of candidates standing for parliament. Surveyors of the history of democracy – including John Keane, in his work *The Life and Death of Democracy*, and Francis Fukuyama, in his two volumes on the history of political order – observe that democracies either innovate or die. Innovation, anyone?

Wanning Sun, you have rather nicely built a strawman and dressed it up as being one of my proposals. Please allow me to knock it down. A couple of quick points. First, I do not object to immigrants from the People's Republic of China. I object to covert agents of influence of a foreign autocracy pretending to embrace Australia's democratic pluralism while devoting themselves to destroying it. Australia's problem is that it has been failing to tell the difference.

Wanning, you ask for evidence. Among other evidence you overlook in *Red Flag* is the well-publicised case of Huang Xiangmo. The billionaire property developer was given permanent residency in Australia, where he set about trying to buy as much influence as possible among Australian politicians and others on behalf of the CCP. He was the donor behind the Sam Dastyari scandal. He was also the donor who tried to use a $400,000 donation to the Labor Party to convince Stephen Conroy to change his policy on China's claims to the South China Sea. The NSW Independent Commission Against Corruption is still working through some of the networks of influence he bought and paid for in the NSW political system on behalf of the United Front Work Department.

Australia eventually cancelled Huang's permanent residency on the grounds that he failed the good character test. He is now persona non grata and the Australian Tax Office is pursing him over $140 million in what it claims to be unpaid taxes. The problem, of course, is that Huang was allowed to live in Australia and operate freely for eight years before being barred.

Australia needs to be better able to detect such people before granting them the immense privilege of free access to our country. The Department of Home Affairs and intelligence agencies evidently lack the skills and resources to do so. I propose that, until they can more reliably sort genuine immigrants from subversive ones, we shift the balance of risk by favouring applicants from Hong Kong and Taiwan over the mainland – because they are more likely to be committed to liberal-democratic principles.

And no, Henry Sherrell, I don't propose a "values test," as you choose to represent it. A quiz on cricket or compulsory voting is not going to filter out subversive foreign agents. I do suggest a more careful sifting of the backgrounds, allegiances and finances of applicants, so that we only admit new citizens who will value our freedoms, not seek to destroy them. I do not propose cutting the intake of ethnic Chinese immigrants. If anything, I propose increasing it. But it must be on condition that they are seeking to become Australians, participants in our liberal democracy, not phony Australians who are here to serve the interests of a foreign autocracy bent on bleeding Australia's sovereignty. Wanning Sun calls this a "discriminatory" immigration policy. I'm certainly not suggesting discriminating on the basis of race. I am suggesting discriminating on the basis of honest intentions and good citizenship. Do you seriously think we should do otherwise, Wanning?

Inaction is not an option. If we don't take prudent measures now, one of two things will happen. Beijing will slowly but surely extend its control over our decision-making systems and we will have surrendered our freedoms without a fight. Or a frustrated Australian electorate will make radical choices at the ballot box and Australia will join its fraternal democracies of the United States and Britain in turning to drastic, populist alternatives that could have ugly consequences.

Enough complacency, enough excuses. The red flag is up. It's time Australia acted on it.

Peter Hartcher

Peter Hartcher is the political and international editor of *The Sydney Morning Herald*. His books include *Bubble Man*, *The Sweet Spot* and *To the Bitter End*. His first Quarterly Essay, *Bipolar Nation*, was published in 2007.

Amy King is a senior lecturer at the Australian National University, specialising in China, Japan and the international relations of the Asia-Pacific region.

Richard McGregor is a senior fellow for East Asia at the Lowy Institute, and the author of two books on China, *The Party* and *Asia's Reckoning*.

Sam Roggeveen is director of the international security program at the Lowy Institute.

Caroline Rosenberg is a psychologist and researcher living in Melbourne.

Henry Sherrell has worked for the Department of Immigration and Citizenship and as a federal member of parliament. He is now a freelance researcher with a focus on Australian immigration policy.

Margaret Simons is an award-winning journalist and the author of thirteen books, including biographies of Malcolm Fraser and Penny Wong. She won the 2015 Walkley Award for Social Equity Journalism and has been honoured with several Quill Awards for journalistic excellence.

Wanning Sun is a professor of media and cultural studies at the University of Technology Sydney, and the author of the 2016 report *Chinese-Language Media in Australia: Developments, Challenges and Opportunities*.

David Walker is the author of *Stranded Nation: White Australia in an Asian Region*.

John West is an adjunct professor at Tokyo's Sophia University and Executive Director of the Asian Century Institute. He has also worked at the Australian Treasury, the OECD and the ADB Institute, and is the author of *Asian Century … on a Knife-Edge*.

QUARTERLY ESSAY
BACK ISSUES

BACK ISSUES: (Prices include GST, postage and handling within Australia.) *Grey indicates out of stock.*

- ☐ **QE 1** ($15.99) Robert Manne *In Denial*
- ☐ **QE 2** ($15.99) John Birmingham *Appeasing Jakarta*
- ☐ **QE 3** ($15.99) Guy Rundle *The Opportunist*
- ☐ **QE 4** ($15.99) Don Watson *Rabbit Syndrome*
- ☐ **QE 5** ($15.99) Mungo MacCallum *Girt By Sea*
- ☐ **QE 6** ($15.99) John Button *Beyond Belief*
- ☐ **QE 7** ($15.99) John Martinkus *Paradise Betrayed*
- ☐ **QE 8** ($15.99) Amanda Lohrey *Groundswell*
- ☐ **QE 9** ($15.99) Tim Flannery *Beautiful Lies*
- ☐ **QE 10** ($15.99) Gideon Haigh *Bad Company*
- ☐ **QE 11** ($15.99) Germaine Greer *Whitefella Jump Up*
- ☐ **QE 12** ($15.99) David Malouf *Made in England*
- ☐ **QE 13** ($15.99) Robert Manne with David Corlett *Sending Them Home*
- ☐ **QE 14** ($15.99) Paul McGeough *Mission Impossible*
- ☐ **QE 15** ($15.99) Margaret Simons *Latham's World*
- ☐ **QE 16** ($15.99) Raimond Gaita *Breach of Trust*
- ☐ **QE 17** ($15.99) John Hirst *'Kangaroo Court'*
- ☐ **QE 18** ($15.99) Gail Bell *The Worried Well*
- ☐ **QE 19** ($15.99) Judith Brett *Relaxed & Comfortable*
- ☐ **QE 20** ($15.99) John Birmingham *A Time for War*
- ☐ **QE 21** ($15.99) Clive Hamilton *What's Left?*
- ☐ **QE 22** ($15.99) Amanda Lohrey *Voting for Jesus*
- ☐ **QE 23** ($15.99) Inga Clendinnen *The History Question*
- ☐ **QE 24** ($15.99) Robyn Davidson *No Fixed Address*
- ☐ **QE 25** ($15.99) Peter Hartcher *Bipolar Nation*
- ☐ **QE 26** ($15.99) David Marr *His Master's Voice*
- ☐ **QE 27** ($15.99) Ian Lowe *Reaction Time*
- ☐ **QE 28** ($15.99) Judith Brett *Exit Right*
- ☐ **QE 29** ($15.99) Anne Manne *Love & Money*
- ☐ **QE 30** ($15.99) Paul Toohey *Last Drinks*
- ☐ **QE 31** ($15.99) Tim Flannery *Now or Never*
- ☐ **QE 32** ($15.99) Kate Jennings *American Revolution*
- ☐ **QE 33** ($15.99) Guy Pearse *Quarry Vision*
- ☐ **QE 34** ($15.99) Annabel Crabb *Stop at Nothing*
- ☐ **QE 35** ($15.99) Noel Pearson *Radical Hope*
- ☐ **QE 36** ($15.99) Mungo MacCallum *Australian Story*
- ☐ **QE 37** ($15.99) Waleed Aly *What's Right?*
- ☐ **QE 38** ($15.99) David Marr *Power Trip*
- ☐ **QE 39** ($15.99) Hugh White *Power Shift*
- ☐ **QE 40** ($15.99) George Megalogenis *Trivial Pursuit*
- ☐ **QE 41** ($15.99) David Malouf *The Happy Life*
- ☐ **QE 42** ($15.99) Judith Brett *Fair Share*
- ☐ **QE 43** ($15.99) Robert Manne *Bad News*
- ☐ **QE 44** ($15.99) Andrew Charlton *Man-Made World*
- ☐ **QE 45** ($15.99) Anna Krien *Us and Them*
- ☐ **QE 46** ($15.99) Laura Tingle *Great Expectations*
- ☐ **QE 47** ($15.99) David Marr *Political Animal*
- ☐ **QE 48** ($15.99) Tim Flannery *After the Future*
- ☐ **QE 49** ($15.99) Mark Latham *Not Dead Yet*
- ☐ **QE 50** ($15.99) Anna Goldsworthy *Unfinished Business*
- ☐ **QE 51** ($15.99) David Marr *The Prince*
- ☐ **QE 52** ($15.99) Linda Jaivin *Found in Translation*
- ☐ **QE 53** ($15.99) Paul Toohey *That Sinking Feeling*
- ☐ **QE 54** ($15.99) Andrew Charlton *Dragon's Tail*
- ☐ **QE 55** ($15.99) Noel Pearson *A Rightful Place*
- ☐ **QE 56** ($15.99) Guy Rundle *Clivosaurus*
- ☐ **QE 57** ($15.99) Karen Hitchcock *Dear Life*
- ☐ **QE 58** ($15.99) David Kilcullen *Blood Year*
- ☐ **QE 59** ($15.99) David Marr *Faction Man*
- ☐ **QE 60** ($15.99) Laura Tingle *Political Amnesia*
- ☐ **QE 61** ($15.99) George Megalogenis *Balancing Act*
- ☐ **QE 62** ($15.99) James Brown *Firing Line*
- ☐ **QE 63** ($15.99) Don Watson *Enemy Within*
- ☐ **QE 64** ($15.99) Stan Grant *The Australian Dream*
- ☐ **QE 65** ($15.99) David Marr *The White Queen*
- ☐ **QE 66** ($15.99) Anna Krien *The Long Goodbye*
- ☐ **QE 67** ($15.99) Benjamin Law *Moral Panic 101*
- ☐ **QE 68** ($15.99) Hugh White *Without America*
- ☐ **QE 69** ($15.99) Mark McKenna *Moment of Truth*
- ☐ **QE 70** ($15.99) Richard Denniss *Dead Right*
- ☐ **QE 71** ($15.99) Laura Tingle *Follow the Leader*
- ☐ **QE 72** ($15.99) Sebastian Smee *Net Loss*
- ☐ **QE 73** ($15.99) Rebecca Huntley *Australia Fair*
- ☐ **QE 74** ($22.99) Erik Jensen *The Prosperity Gospel*
- ☐ **QE 75** ($22.99) Annabel Crabb *Men at Work*
- ☐ **QE 76** ($22.99) Peter Hartcher *Red Flag*

NAME:

ADDRESS:

EMAIL: PHONE:

Please include this form with payment details overleaf.

☐ **ONE-YEAR AUTO-RENEWING PRINT AND DIGITAL SUBSCRIPTION: $69.95***
REQUIRES EMAIL & CREDIT CARD, 4 issues, receive 24% off the cover price

☐ **TWO-YEAR PRINT AND DIGITAL SUBSCRIPTION: $149.95** 8 issues

☐ **ONE-YEAR AUTO-RENEWING PRINT AND DIGITAL INTERNATIONAL SUBSCRIPTION: $109.95***
REQUIRES EMAIL & CREDIT CARD, 4 issues

☐ **ONE-YEAR DIGITAL ONLY SUBSCRIPTION: $49.95** REQUIRES EMAIL, 4 issues

☐ **ONE-YEAR PRINT AND DIGITAL GIFT SUBSCRIPTION: $79.95** 4 issues, receive 13% off the cover price. Subscriptions outside Australia **$119.95**

☐ **TWO-YEAR PRINT AND DIGITAL GIFT SUBSCRIPTION $149.95** 8 issues, receive 13% off the cover price

☐ TICK HERE TO COMMENCE SUBSCRIPTION WITH THE CURRENT ISSUE

SUBSCRIBER'S NAME:

ADDRESS:

EMAIL: PHONE:

RECIPIENT'S NAME:

ADDRESS:

EMAIL: PHONE:

PAYMENT DETAILS: Enclose a cheque/money order made out to Schwartz Books Pty Ltd.
Or debit my credit card (MasterCard, Visa and Amex accepted).
Freepost: Quarterly Essay, Reply Paid 90094, Carlton VIC 3053
All prices include GST, postage and handling.

CARD NO. ☐☐☐☐☐☐☐☐☐☐☐☐☐☐☐☐

EXPIRY DATE: / CCV: AMOUNT: $

PURCHASER'S NAME: SIGNATURE:

PURCHASER'S EMAIL:

Subscribe online at **quarterlyessay.com/subscribe** • Freecall: 1800 077 514 • Phone: 03 9486 0288
Email: subscribe@quarterlyessay.com (please do not send electronic scans of this form)

* Your subscription will automatically renew until you notify us to stop. Prior to the end of your subscription period, we will send you a reminder notice that will indicate the renewal price. If you do not notify us to stop the renewal, your credit or debit card will automatically be charged for the same period. You may notify us to stop the renewal via the account dashboard or by contacting us. Australian subscriptions only.